# One thousand years of
# ENGLISH CHURCH MONUMENTS

# One thousand years of
# ENGLISH CHURCH MONUMENTS

## Edited by Sally Badham

*Ecclesiology Today* · Issue 43 · December 2010

ISSN: 1460-4213
ISBN: 978-0-946823-14-7

Published 2010 by the Ecclesiological Society
c/o The Society of Antiquaries of London
Burlington House
Piccadilly
London
WIV 0HS

The Ecclesiological Society is a registered charity.
Charity No. 210501.

www.ecclsoc.org

The views expressed in this publication are those of the authors, and do not necessarily represent those of the Ecclesiological Society or its officers.

*Front cover:* Detail of the tomb monument to Lady Dorothea Dodderidge (1614) at Exeter Cathedral, discussed in the article by Paul Cockerham.
*Back cover:* Detail of the monument to Louisa Blanche Foljambe and Frederick (1871) by William Calder Marshall, at St Mary's, Tickhill, Yorkshire, discussed in the article by Jane Kelsall.
*Both photographs by C B Newham*

# Ecclesiology Today

*Journal of the
Ecclesiological Society*

Issue 43
published December 2010

# Contents

# Chairman's letter

Dear Fellow Member

## *Ecclesiology Today*

This edition of *Ecclesiology Today* is devoted to English church monuments. As Sally Badham, our guest editor, explains in her introduction, its genesis was an email conversation from nearly two years ago. I am delighted how that germ of an idea has grown into this substantial volume, and the Society is grateful both for Sally's vision and energy in seeing it through, and for the efforts of the group of expert contributors she persuaded to write for us. Between them I believe they have produced a volume which should be of interest to all who love churches, whether or not their particular interest lies in church monuments.

As members know, it is the intention that we produce two issues of *Ecclesiology Today* per year. This is the second edition for 2010. Our next issue (no. 44) is due out half way through 2011, and will be the first to be produced by our new Hon. Editor, Dr Lynne Broughton. Lynne is keen to receive offers of articles, so please contact her if you would like to submit a piece: she is happy to talk matters through at a very early stage.

## *Presidency*

As already known to those who attended our Annual General Meeting in October, after many years service Dr Donald Buttress has resigned as President of the Society. At the Annual Conference immediately preceding the AGM I was able to say a few words of thanks, emphasising the active interest he has shown in the Society and the personal support he has given, and to present him with a small token of our gratitude. I am glad to say that he is retaining his links with the Society by becoming a Vice-President.

For those not at the AGM, I am pleased to be able to announce that our new President is the Right Reverend David Stancliffe, recently-retired Bishop of Salisbury. He will be known to many members already. To appreciate some of his ecclesiological interests, a look at his recent *The Lion Companion to Church Architecture* (Oxford, 2008) is recommended, a *tour de force* which describes churches from a range of geographies, periods and confessions, and is notable for discussing the architecture of churches in the context of their use and purpose. We are delighted that he has accepted our invitation to be President.

Trevor Cooper
Chairman of Council

# Church Monuments: about this issue

*Sally Badham*

OFF-HAND REMARKS can have unexpected consequences. This I found early in 2009 when I submitted an article to *Ecclesiology Today* about the commemoration in brass and glass of the Blackburn family of York and their kin. I commented to Trevor Cooper (this was before the Society had appointed its new Editor) that I hoped it would be of interest, although I had rarely seen articles about church monuments in the journal. Trevor replied:

> Your comment that we don't often carry material on monuments has got me thinking, whether we ought to have a themed issue on the subject . . . it might be that our style of journal could do something useful in a themed issue in a way which the house style of [the] Church Monuments Society journal would find more difficult.

After more discussion and with the enthusiastic support of the councils of the Ecclesiological Society and the Church Monuments Society, I accepted an invitation to act as guest editor for an issue of *Ecclesiology Today* devoted to the topic of church monuments.

Perhaps the most difficult part of the challenge was to decide which approach to adopt when commissioning articles for this special edition. As I understand it, perhaps about a tenth of Ecclesiological Society members have a specific interest in church monuments. Most of you will have noticed monuments while you explore churches but perhaps not have paid them as much attention as, say, the architecture, glass, woodwork or other fittings. It was therefore clear that what was required was not a miscellany of individual essays aimed at those already deeply interested in the subject, but a structured series of tasters accessible to the intelligent non-specialist, which those whose curiosity is piqued can follow up through the sources quoted in the references.

My first aim, therefore, in commissioning contributions for this edition was to show you what monuments have to offer to those with interests in other aspects of churches by providing a cohesive themed volume that would cover monuments from the pre-Conquest period to the twentieth century. A comprehensive history of church monuments is not intended; instead contributors have chosen particular issues and approaches which they hope will have general appeal. Their essays cover only a tiny part of the subject, which has a huge scope. Most concern intra-mural monuments, but the final article demonstrates that churchyard monuments also can be extremely interesting. All contributors have focused primarily on English monuments, but there are also many fascinating memorials in Scotland, Wales, Ireland, continental Europe and beyond.

My second aim was to provide a variety of perspectives and show how monuments can inform a wide variety of studies. Contributors include art historians, church archaeologists, historians, literary scholars and, to modify the Ecclesiological Society's slogan, those who just love church monuments. Some who have contributed to this volume have spent their working lives in academia or museums, while others (like me) have had to regard the study of monuments as a leisure interest, albeit a somewhat consuming one. (This is not to say that those in the first group should be regarded as professionals and the second amateurs, as all those who have contributed to this volume are recognised authorities in their field.)

The Ecclesiological Society Council approved my list of authors and subjects, but, just when I was feeling that all was nicely under control, threw me a curved ball. I heard that:

> It would be very interesting (if possible) to have an introductory chapter which talked about the role and place of monuments in church buildings over the centuries, their location, their purpose, and perhaps ask questions about how (if at all) they were explicitly incorporated into the liturgy.

My first reaction was that to do even moderate justice to such a broad brief would take at least one whole issue of *Ecclesiology Today*, and could hardly be contained in just a few thousand words. It would also need to be written by someone with an exceptionally wide interest in monuments. If I were to deliver, all would all depend on finding someone who would rise to any challenge, even a seeming 'Mission Impossible' like this. Well, I persuaded someone to take it on and I am glad to say that the resulting essay delivers all that was asked for and provides the perfect backdrop to the rest of the volume.

I am deeply grateful to all those who have contributed to this special issue of *Ecclesiology Today*. I hope their work will generate a greater interest in and understanding of church monuments. Needless to say, the views expressed are those of the various authors and should not be taken necessarily to represent the views of the Ecclesiological Society (or even the guest editor).

# The Church Monuments Society

Although, as explained above, the contributors to this volume come from a wide variety of backgrounds and adopt a range of approaches to the study of church monuments, they have in common an active involvement in the Church Monuments Society. The CMS promotes the study, care, appreciation and conservation of church monuments through a lively and varied programme of meetings, study visits and publications. Members' interests vary from simple cross slabs to large and elaborate effigial monuments, both in the UK and abroad. The society offers a unique opportunity for people to meet and exchange views on a subject which spans many disciplines including art history, genealogy, political and social history, as well as costume, armour and heraldry.

Current membership rates are £20 individual, £30 corporate and £15 (full-time) student, with the subscription year running from 1 June to 31 May. Joining the CMS will offer the following benefits:

– the journal *Church Monuments*. Published once a year, typically at least 144 pages in length and richly illustrated (including colour plates), this peer reviewed journal attracts articles from both professional scholars and informed enthusiasts. It also has an extensive reviews section.

– *CMS Newsletter*. This informal publication is produced twice a year and contains short articles on monuments, information about forthcoming activities, work in progress, lists of new publications on monuments, and related topics.

– the opportunity to attend biennial weekend symposia, annual study days at churches rich in monuments, coach excursions, ad-hoc lecture meetings and other events.

To find out more, visit the website www.churchmonuments society.org or contact the Hon. Membership Secretary, Dr Clive Easter, 55 Bowden Park Road, Crownhill, Plymouth, PL6 5NG.

# Lineage, Liturgy and Locus: the changing role of English funeral monuments

*Paul Cockerham*

IN A REMARKABLY diverse and seminal collection of epitaphs published in 1631, John Weever aimed 'to publish to the view of the world, as well the moderne, as the ancient memorialls of the dead'. Additionally, he would have 'gained as much as I looke for, if I shall draw others, when I am dead, into this argument; whose inquisitive diligence and learning may finde out more, and amend mine'.[1] Picking up Weever's gauntlet of finding out more, we need to look beyond his epitaphs to determine the very function of a monument at the time it was erected. How, for instance, did a monument relate to its contemporary context, both in its selected location and its inclusion in rituals and liturgy? And how did this involvement develop over time? This paper aims to respond to these questions not by skimming through a broad chronological history[2] but adopting instead a comparative methodology, contextualising individual monuments at periods on a timeline extending from late medieval to the Enlightenment.

## Medieval monuments

Tomb monuments originated as plain stone slabs laid flat in a churchyard to act as grave markers, and incised with simple cross designs developed from the decorated lids of sarcophagi and stone coffins. From these early medieval stones developed internal floor monuments of increasing design complexity and size, such that by the late medieval period they incorporated effigies of the deceased, perhaps in gilded brass, within lavish architectural enclosures and with other accessories. Three-dimensional monuments evolved concurrently, by the late medieval period comprising large tomb chests with sculpted effigies of the deceased on top and imagery on the sides, occasionally set inside enormous architectural structures.

Common to all late medieval monuments, however, were three things. Their primary purpose was to be noticed. As a direct sequela they were commissioned to elicit prayers for the commemorated to accelerate the process by which their soul(s) were refined in Purgatory before they entered Heaven. Additionally, the monument was a statement of how the deceased wished to be remembered, manifesting their status and lordly authority. These purposes were exemplified through visual imagery and texts.

To take a case study, the tomb of Bishop Edmund Stafford (1419) in Exeter Cathedral, Devon, comprises his alabaster figure

*Paul Cockerham is a Fellow of the Society of Antiquaries of London and a Vice-President of the Monumental Brass Society.*

beautifully sculpted in complete episcopal dress, with his hands reverentially at prayer (Fig. 1). There is a small alabaster 'gablette' placed over his head, with this and the effigy resting on an elaborate heraldic tomb chest with an ornate stone canopy above and a short verse inscription on the side. [3] So much for the monument itself, but its function can only properly be assessed within the context of the other commemorative strategies planned by the bishop. He ordered the tomb himself, specifying its location on the south side of St John's chapel at the east end of the north choir aisle, so imposing his own commemorative artefact on an important sacred space. [4] Additionally, Stafford endowed the chapel with two chantry priests, celebrating for the souls of himself, his father, mother and uncle, kinsmen, Sir Humphrey Stafford, King Henry IV and his sons. [5] As the tomb was open on the south side to the body of the Lady Chapel, structurally it mirrored the earlier tomb of bishop Bronescombe (1280) on the south side, which was much embellished in the fifteenth century to make the resemblance closer still (Fig. 2). The Lady Chapel was at the heart of the Cathedral, dedicated to the Virgin Mary, and was where at least three daily masses were said, to which lay worshippers were admitted. [6] The sentiment of prayers for the dead recited in the Lady Chapel cannot fail to have been influenced by the large tombs to these two bishops, flanking the entrance, as well as the gravestone of Bishop Quivil (1291) in the centre of the chapel itself. [7] Hence, the figure of Bishop Stafford would have acted as a visible aide-mémoire for personal inclusion in these cycles of intercessory prayer, and the heraldic relationships symbolised on the tomb chest's sides would have ensured the perpetual commemoration of an even wider family. [8]

Furthermore, it is hardly coincidental that Stafford's monument is in line with the arcade of the north wall of the Lady Chapel and the tombs of earlier bishops which had been transposed there, [9] ensuring that Stafford was visibly encompassed within the corporate body of his predecessors – the establishment bishopric. Sponsored exclusivity of high status private prayer for himself and his family took place within his own chantry chapel. Yet simultaneously this audience was widened, not only because these private masses were probably observed by lay persons circulating around the chancel aisles, [10] but also because the strategic position of Stafford's tomb relative to the others in the Lady Chapel made sure that he was remembered as part of the greater *ecclesia*.

This corporate memory was further enhanced by the proximity to the bishop's tomb of the graveslab to one of his household, Canon William Langeton (1414). [11] His modest but

*Fig. 1: Exeter Cathedral, Devon, effigy from the tomb monument of Bishop Edmund Stafford (1419). Photo: C B Newham*

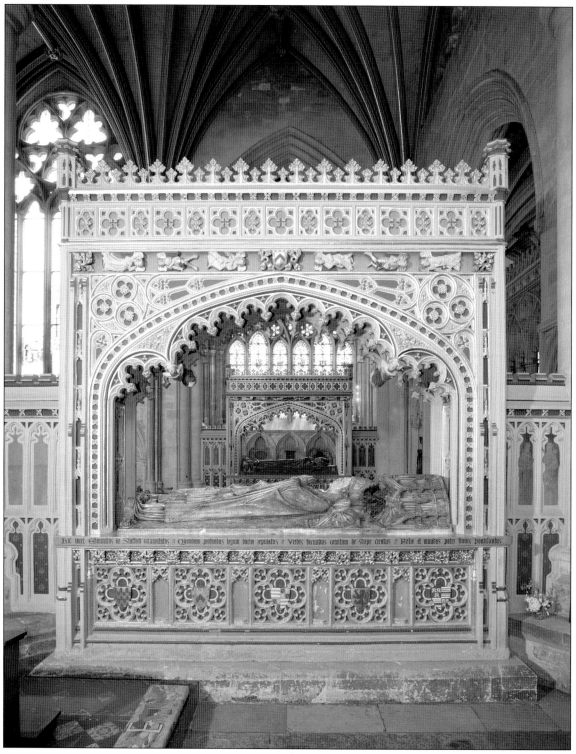

*Fig. 2: Exeter Cathedral, tomb monument of Bishop Edmund Stafford (1419) with that of Bishop Walter Bronescombe (1280) in the background. Photo: C B Newham*

evocative tombstone (Fig. 3) bears a small brass showing him in profile, kneeling, and with his head tilted upwards following the line of a precatory scroll which bears a responsary from the Office of the Dead.[12] Below the figure is a formulaic inscription seeking prayers for the soul and supplemented to highlight Langeton's kinship with the bishop. Consequently, both this, the Stafford arms at the corners of the slab and the family knot incorporated into the orphreys of his cope, all combine to maximise the spectator's awareness of Langeton's obligation to Stafford. Langeton willed that he should be buried 'either on the right or to the left of the tomb of Bishop Stafford'[13] and so he was, his graveslab lying to the north of Stafford's tomb on the floor of St John's chapel. He kneels towards the recumbent figure of his bishop and relative, the responsary on his brass scroll resonating to the sixth lesson of Matins as if it had been read by the bishop himself. Not only would the brass have ensured that Langeton's soul was remembered by those able to understand and respond to the

*Fig. 3: Exeter Cathedral, monumental brass of Canon William Langeton (1413). Photo: C B Newham*

message of the inscription, as well as at his month's mind and anniversary,[14] but there was a much closer link, with Langeton's words continually recited by bishop Stafford's chantry priests in the ritual performance of their duties. All these devices – Langeton humbly depicted at prayer for his own salvation as well as for his bishop, the heraldic and textual reminders of kinship, and the phrase from a mass for the dead used as a verbal mnemonic – closely interlocked to maximise the intercessory value of his brass as a function of imagery and location. The mutuality of these two monuments is quite clear; their particular intimacy was obviously sanctioned by Stafford himself.

Medieval funeral monuments were also incorporated into more lavish and personal iconographic programmes, such as the Speke chantry (Fig. 4) in the north choir aisle of the cathedral,[15] equally symbolic of wider schemes of memorialisation. For instance, in 1438 John Stourton the elder, of Preston, Somerset, willed his body to be buried in Stavordale Priory, and also:

*Fig. 4: Exeter Cathedral, chantry chapel of Sir John Speke (1518). Photo: C B Newham*

that the church of Staverdale and the cloister there shall be completed in all things, as well in glazing the windows as in other buildings there to be done … I will that two images carried thither by me shall be ordained and placed in the middle of the choir of the said church, between the stalls there, and that underneath shall be made a certain tomb, ordained and walled for the bodies of me and my wife … with one closet of iron bars around the said tomb; and that the reading desk shall be at the head of the said tomb. Item, I will that the aforesaid church shall be throughout honestly paved with 'Tyle' of my arms and the arms of my mother.[16]

The rebuilding of the priory was completed in 1443 and one can only now imagine the heraldically-saturated and prestigious setting of the tomb and its accessories within the choir. On a lesser scale, in 1469 Walter Sydenham Esq. wanted to be buried at Brympton, Somerset, and in addition he willed 'to the High aulter … one paire of Aulter Clothes of Crimesyne Damask with a Frontille of blak velvet embrawded. Item I bequethe xxs. of peise grotes to make a boxe to put in oure lordes body and to honge over the said aulter. Item I bequethe to the maytenaunce of a lampe to brenne a fore our lordes body at the said aulter'.[17]

These more transitory elements of intercessory schemes were abandoned or consolidated through insufficient endowment to maintain them, or they were sold on and/or destroyed as a result of the final Chantries act of 1547. So although nowadays monuments have been stripped of many of their contemporary intercessory accessories, their original locations are instructive as to how they might have functioned liturgically. Commemoration of the dead had come to focus on the funeral mass, and those subsequent masses, which enacted the doctrine of transubstantiation. The consecrated bread and wine, elevated over the altar at the very crux of the ritual, were transformed into the body and blood of Christ, so that intercessory prayers were made in His very presence and in consequence carried more weight.[18] Hence, Richard Bruton, canon of Wells (1417) willed that 'One small *tabula* at the time of mass to be placed before the priest's eyes, whereon shall be written, *Orate pro anima Ricardi Bruton parentumque eius et omnium animarum pro quibus tenetur'*.[19]

A tomb could equally intrude itself into sacred space and ritual, enabling the commemorated to benefit from a perception of sanctity. The north side of the chancel was a particularly desirable position: firstly, it was near to where the Gospel was read; secondly, it was also close to one of the principal images of the church; and lastly, it was the position usually occupied by the Easter sepulchre, this last enhancing the relationship of the commemorated with the suffering of Christ.[20] Similar holy locations were also popular. Henry Burnell Esq. (1490) wanted to be buried 'in the myddys of the high aulter, so that my body may ligh part underneath the same aulter, so that the Mynesters of Crist that shall say masses ther may stond upon my body while they shall mynester the blyssed sacrament of our Lordes body'.[21] Some wished to be memorialised before the image of a particular favourite saint, or in front of the Rood;[22] others desired to be buried in the porch by the stoup, or by the church door,[23] which may appear to have been humble locations relative to the holiest parts of the church. Paradoxically however, these were the areas where people congregated, and monuments located there would have been highly visible. In particular, those entering and leaving the church would have paused by the stoup and blessed themselves with holy water, reciting a personal prayer as they did so, making this location an astute choice for siting a monument there, inviting an extension to that personal invocation. With time burial location both inside and outside the church became increasingly specified, so it was this link between spiritual remembrance and liturgy which concerned many testators more than their social memory conveyed by any monumental imagery, which may anyway have been commissioned by the deceased's executors. Hence, social aspirations may well have been secondary to the spiritual benefits mediated by a tomb.[24]

In a small number of cases imagery was selected which amplified the relationship between the deceased, their monument, and liturgy.[25] A few brasses clearly refer to the Judgement and the resurrection of the body, with a poignant example at Lavenham, Suffolk to Thomas Spryng and family (1486) (Fig. 5). The figures of Thomas, his wife and their children are all depicted in shrouds and emerging from two coffins with their lids pushed aside, with precatory scrolls rising towards a (lost) plate presumably of Christ sitting in Judgement upon them. While remarkable in itself the location of the brass is equally telling. Spryng was a rich but non-armigerous clothier and burial close to the main altar may have been socially unattainable. What better solution than to build a 'vestibularium', where he was buried, attached to the east end of the chancel? This unpretentious location matched the humility with which he was represented on his tomb, yet it was close to the high altar and continually mindful to the priest whom he paid to say masses for him.[26]

This amalgamation of medieval monuments into the church fabric highlights their need to be contextualised among the other commissioned artefacts of remembrance. Initially these commemorative processes encompassed only the nobility, gentry and higher clergy, but by the early sixteenth century they symbolised an integration between the church and the middling

*Fig. 5: Lavenham, Suffolk, monumental brass of Thomas Spryng and family (1486). Photo: reproduced by courtesy of the late Malcolm Norris*

sort of people, as burial and tomb commemoration became cheaper and more commonly permitted. Monuments were more affordable – by now a small brass inscription in its slab could be had for a mere ten shillings[27] – and there were also large numbers of them in many churches. Generations of the major manorial families might have colonised specific areas of a church with successive tombs, but intra-mural burial and monument erection elsewhere in the church gradually incorporated a much broader cross-section of parish society. This would have enlarged further still as the wider families of those commemorated by monuments were actively involved in intercessions for their dead relatives. However, the fundamental doctrinal changes which were imposed in the mid-sixteenth century, particularly the termination of all intercessory activity, dramatically shifted the rationale behind the erection of a tomb monument to one which was politically and religiously acceptable to the establishment.[28]

## Post-Reformation funeral monuments
In a directive to halt the monument destruction resulting from this official change in religious orthodoxy, Elizabeth I's proclamation of 1560 identified the effects of such iconoclasm,

which had extinguished 'the honourable and good memory of sundry virtuous and noble persons deceased … also the true understanding of divers families in this realm (who have descended of the blood of the same persons deceased) is thereby so darkened as the true course of their inheritance may be hereafter interrupted'.[29]

So what, now, was the function of a monument? Protestant theology insisted that the soul of the deceased was despatched immediately after death, inducing an abrupt separation between the living and the dead. Hence, a monument was now primarily a permanent marker of a dead individual, symbolising the continued presence of that person and linking him with a lineage of both ancestors and descendants, which emphasised and maintained that family's status, representing a social continuum at a time when a landed descent was fractured. While this was also one of the purposes of a pre-Reformation monument, of which the imagery and text exemplified status and family lineage alongside the more important salvitic elements of the design, monuments were now being erected at a time of unprecedented activity in the land market and when family tensions were high as their traditional religious privileges and rituals were acutely challenged. By the 1560s the need was for a funeral monument which was religiously anodyne. Instead of inviting prayer like their medieval counterparts, albeit many of which remained undisturbed close by, these Elizabethan structures encompassed the new orthodoxy by encouraging an understanding of salvation achieved through living virtuously, their inscriptions providing exemplars based on the lives of those commemorated.[30]

Continuing the Exeter examples, the tomb of Sir Gawen Carew (1589) dominates St John's chapel (Fig. 6). It is an enormous structure, comprising a table bearing the sculpted relief figures of Sir Gawen and his second wife; over them is a large canopy supported by Corinthian columns and pilasters, with panels bearing shields enclosing the back and sides and more sculptural and heraldic exuberance above. Under the table is a third full-size figure, of Sir Peter Carew, Sir Gawen's nephew, peculiarly depicted in a cross-legged pose, inclined slightly towards the spectator and with his hand grasping his sword.[31] The original inscriptions are now lost, but the three remaining visual discourses of the tomb – architecture, effigies and heraldry – are still overwhelming. Powerful, elaborately decorated classical architecture forms a precise, rigid frame to the monument. The quasi-linear principal effigies are uncompromisingly recumbent inside it, not a fold of drapery out of place, and with their hands at prayer are beseeching their salvation. There is an intense contrast with the twisted effigy below whose pose connotes

*Fig. 6: Exeter Cathedral, tomb monument of Sir Gawen Carew (1598), his wife and nephew. Photo: C B Newham*

'longevity and continuity and perhaps referred to the statues of kings and prophets displayed on facades such as those on Exeter cathedral itself or the figures set out at the base of representations of the Tree of Jesse, the father of all ancestral imagery'.[32] The profusion of heraldry – forty-three shields in all – is set vertically to maximise its visual impact.

But what does this tomb mean? Sir Gawen left detailed instructions in his will, requesting 'a Toombe to be made and sett over my bodye', going on to spell out in detail the heraldry, genealogy and social status of his wives and their former husbands that he wanted represented on it.[33] The consequent superabundance of heraldry specifically and permanently articulated Carew's connections during his lifetime at Court, perpetuating after his death his status in local and wider society. It inferred a venerable and élite lineage, Sir Peter's subsidiary figure resonating in this antiquity; yet his tortured posture was equally a metaphor for the conflict of a military Protestant ethic, in the sustained fight against Catholicism which dogmatised Elizabethan court society. In contrast, serene and contemplative above, the effigies of Sir Gawen and his wife exemplified the dead in life, crystallising their achievements in living a godly life as well as providing the spectator with symbols of continuity which negated the horror of death and the potential change in social harmony. Their presence bridged the presumed crisis of succession from one (dead) generation to the next (living) one by the stereotypical quietude of the effigies: their very permanence communicated a reassuring aura of the perpetuity of the social order.[34]

Yet without a spectator to comprehend this monument, at whatever level of understanding, there would have been little purpose in its erection. Location was just as crucial post-Reformation as pre-Reformation, and, with the liturgical changes consequent upon Protestantism, a lay hierarchy of social space in a church suppressed the traditional ecclesiastical one. Elizabethan Protestants were, theoretically, immune to the idea and practice of burial close to a holy place, such as the altar, as it now induced no spiritual advantage. The location of the Carew monuments within St John's chapel suggests a desired exclusivity harking back to its original function as a chantry chapel for Bishop Stafford, which ceased in 1548, yet the tomb was also quite visible to people walking by in the choir aisles and the Lady Chapel. In many churches the removal of the rood screen maximised the potential visibility of monuments in the chancel. Manorial lords lost no time in commissioning enormous, grandiose tombs and setting them up in chancels, some even taking over the position of the high altar, commanding that newly opened out space and controlling the view that the parishioners enjoyed into it.[35] Thus, location reinforced the functions of these monuments, smoothing over potential inheritance crises in a dominating manorial descent and reassuring parishioners by maintaining a social regularity. They combined with grand manorial pews to buttress that family's perceived status in an increasingly educated, articulate and opportunist society, acting together as part of a defence strategy against potential manorial and governmental hubris.

Burial alongside earlier generations of the same family was a commonplace request in Elizabethan wills therefore. Commemoration of ancestors continued without interruption, hence chantry chapels were converted into private family chapels or appropriated by succeeding families.[36] In Exeter cathedral Lady Dorothea Dodderidge (1614) negotiated successfully to erect her tomb at the east end of the Lady Chapel, at the theological crux of the cathedral and its traditional Marian veneration, as well as at the core of the greater *ecclesia*, among the bishops' tombs.[37] It was balanced by the monument to her husband Sir John Dodderidge (1628) on the opposite side of the high altar, so they visually appropriated the east end of the chapel.[38] This 'pairing' of monuments was established early on in Exeter with the bishops' tombs, so in choosing the sites of their own tombs the Dodderidges, perhaps unconsciously, perpetuated a pre-Reformation custom. In addition they commissioned monuments whose qualities resonated with those of the bishops as they all comprised finely dressed figures raised up on tomb chests, elaborated with heraldry and inscriptions inside an architectural superstructure.[39] Yet while the bishops are peacefully recumbent, Lady Dodderidge is propped up on one elbow and casts her melancholic gaze across the body of the chapel at the tomb of her husband (Fig. 7). This affinity reflected the mutuality between the tombs of Bishops Stafford and Bronescombe in particular, which flanked the entrance to the Chapel.

A continuity in customs affecting monument erection was also manifest in other ways.[40] The persistent use of a funeral pall and of lights, the inclusion of the poor in funeral processions and bequests to them, were all common to both pre- and post-Reformation burials. From the late sixteenth century onwards the preaching of a theologically erudite funeral sermon was frequently accompanied by an elegy about the deceased, which if repeated after a month and a year may have been seen to mimic the pre-Reformation prayers for the soul(s) of the departed, as in the month's mind and anniversary. As Margaret Rampston, widow, of Chingford, Essex, stated in 1590, 'I will that Dr Andrewes [vicar of Chigwell] may be entreated to make my funeral and month's

*Fig. 7: Exeter Cathedral, tomb monument of Lady Dorothea Dodderidge (1614). Photo: C B Newham*

sermon'.[41] Similarly, John Felgate, yeoman, of Stonham Aspal, Suffolk, willed in 1623 that his executrix 'procure 8 sermons [in separate parishes] namely 1 sermon at burial, 1 sermon on that day a 12 month & so successively for 6 more years'.[42] Yet all these rituals related chiefly to the funeral. Once the body had been buried a monument erected over it was frequently the only token of the life and death of that individual. That said, the sermon preached in 1619 at the funeral of Mrs Elizabeth Juxon in St Laurence Pountney, London, was subsequently published as *The Monument or Tombe-Stone*. By 1631 it had gone into five editions, implying an acknowledged bond between the temporary nature of the funeral and the perpetuity of a monument. Affirmation of the life and death of an individual modulated from verbal ceremony to silent rhetoric therefore; as the 1566 will of Thomas Myldmay esquire of Moulsham insisted, 'My executors shall bestow [£40] upon a comely tomb or monument of hard stone … as a remembrance of our being here together upon this earth and for a remembrance to our children and friends left behind us, without any pomp or glory or other respect'.[43]

These changes signalled a significant reduction, to the point of separation, in the relationship between a tomb and liturgy; it was almost as if there were a secular detachment of the monument from religion. However, Finch has traced epitaphs which mimicked the funeral sermon and were frequently in tune with Protestant theology,[44] and monuments may also have promulgated a Protestant identity: kneeling effigies were common, but they now faced a prayer desk with the Bible open upon it, and with the family rather than the individual providing the model (Fig. 8). Other means of recall also evolved. In Cornwall for example, numerous slate monuments were erected on the walls of the church, the homogenous, grey-black stone contrasting starkly with the newly whitened, evangelical church interiors, stripped of religious clutter and decoration. White and black are absolute, simple colours. White 'Consisteth of very much Light'; Black, the colour of slate, represented 'the Horror of Death and Corruption'.[45] Mural slate monuments would have increasingly dominated the ordered reconstruction of these bare church 'halls', the visual contrast and developing pattern of dark slates on light walls establishing itself as a permanent imprint on the minds of the parishioners. The harsh but complementary visual clash of black (Death) on white (Life) moves radically on from memory perpetuated by specific medieval imagery, to one formed not from an individual's monument but one manifest as an evolving, mnemonic pattern of the entire mass of the slate slabs and their wholesale commemoration.

*Fig. 8: North Hill, Cornwall, mural slate slab of Thomas Vincent (1606) and family. Photo: Paul Cockerham*

The role of a monument had evolved rapidly, with its impact attested to at several levels. Every spectator would appreciate the large scale, grandeur and overwhelming dominance of a tomb and what it said about the commemorated. Most would understand the heraldry, and if not recognising all of it then they would at least recall by its very complexity how well connected with other armigerous families the commemorated individual was. The sculpted figures of the deceased acted as a permanent visible reminder of their original presence and social role; and the inscriptions, sometimes very sophisticated and appreciated only by a few, moved these structures into an altogether higher plane of élite recognition and appreciation. Yet these discourses were also being encompassed by other social milieu. Family portraiture was well established, with successive generations of heads of families 'hung' in their solars, although only as a private contrivance of continuity of succession.[46] Civic portraits were commissioned for town and livery company halls, creating separate lineages of leadership as a cause for celebration and self-satisfaction in their success – but all ultimately removing schemes of memorialisation from a liturgical setting.[47]

## The Romantic period

The following centuries maintained the momentum of this secularisation. Funeral monuments continued to proliferate in churches as manorial families crammed them into any remaining space in their family chapels. Where traditional architectural structures were now spatially impossible, hanging wall monuments superseded, with busts of the deceased and allegorical symbols of the Virtues and of mortality. Complicated texts and heraldic metaphors were introduced, the effects of which were to reduce the panoply of a monument, but only, paradoxically, as a means of contrasting this self-effacement with the exalted achievements of the deceased that they extolled.[48] Where space did permit, imagery replaced architecturally based structures with vibrant dramas of family life and allegory, but crucially they all still retained the message of lineage and status. The arrival in England of sculptors of the calibre of Rysbrack, Scheemakers and Roubiliac moved funerary sculpture into a different art form as an increasingly aesthetic appreciation of these sculptures evolved. The surface finish of monuments, for example, became an important aspect of quality in an age when a steadily increasing range of luxury goods was available to the consumer.[49] This realisation helped to distance monuments from their earlier liturgical function; indeed, the enormous and complicated dramatic composition planned by Roubiliac for the monument to Richard Boyle, Viscount Shannon (1757) at Walton-on-Thames, Surrey, was so obviously inappropriate for the church that he recommended it to be erected in a specially built extension, so that it might be viewed for its own sake – a splendid public military heroism blended with family emotionalism, grief and an atmosphere of melancholy.[50]

A last case study is provided by the monument to Admiral Edward Boscawen (1763) which was erected in the estate church of St Michael Penkivel, Cornwall (Fig. 9). An early nineteenth-century historian reverently described the 'stately altar tomb, formed of beautifully polished marble, on the top of which is a remarkably fine bust of the deceased, surrounded by a variety of implements connected with naval warfare'.[51] The epitaph was composed by Boscawen's 'intellectual' wife in forty-five lines of English prose which exemplify the flawless personal qualities of the admiral: 'His concern for the interest, and unwearied attention to the health of all under his command, softened the necessary exactions of duty, and the rigors [sic] of discipline, by the care of a guardian, and the tenderness of a father'.[52]

What is peculiar, however, is that this remotely sited monument was a family's unequivocal response to a lack of governmental interest, despite public demand, in commissioning a

monument for the admiral in a more ostentatious location such as Westminster Abbey.[53] Despite his father, the first Viscount Falmouth being buried at St Michael's in 1733, this was the first Boscawen monument erected there since 1626, when an enigmatic effigial tomb was put up by Hugh Boscawen Esq. to commemorate several earlier generations of the family back to 1559.[54] This earlier monument was a modulation of an individual memorial into a symbol of dynastic commemoration, which perhaps came to signify its contemporary function forwards in time as much as it celebrated the Boscawens retrospectively. It took a man of great political reputation, the naval hero of the battle of Louisburg, to break with this symbolism when he was buried at St Michael's 'amidst the groans and tears of his beloved Cornishmen'.[55] The monument was a signed collaborative effort

*Fig. 10: St Michael Penkivel, mural commemorative tablet to Edward Hugh Boscawen (1774). Photo: Paul Cockerham*

EDWARD HUGH BOSCAWEN *Esq.*
Eldeſt Son of Admiral *BOSCAWEN*
and of *FRANCES* his Wife.
Died alas! in the flower of his Age:
At the Spa in *GERMANY*
His Remains were brought over, to be
interr'd near thoſe of his illuſtrious Father.
He was twice elected Repreſentative
in PARLIAMENT for the Borough of *TRURO*
Born 13.ᵗ Sep. O.S.1744. Died 17.ᵗ July. 1774.

between Robert Adam, the classical architect involved at the admiral's house at Hatchlands, Surrey, and the by then ageing sculptor Michael Rysbrack.[56] Despite the artist's infirmity the detail on the monument is crisp, and the realism of the bust portrait, set against the pyramid background, utterly convincing. Equally, the austere classicalism of design was symbolic of the physical and moral advances by which the élite sought to differentiate themselves from the lower orders. This monument, moreover, quickly stimulated more monuments to family members, all relatively standardised tablets by Joseph Nollekens (Fig. 10), which reinforced the Boscawen colonisation of the church, and by employing the same dark pyramidal background echoed the Admiral's monument. Indeed, as prior to its restoration in 1862 the church was noted as being decorated like a domestic family house, it is hard to avoid the sense of complete secular control of this church building and its contents, symbolised by the combination of domestic architect and monumental sculptor for the admiral's tomb. Services in the church would have been seen perhaps as secondary to the overwhelming presence of the family's funeral monuments; these promoted a civic, national pride, imbued with qualities reflecting heroism, a national supremacy, defeat of the enemy and a pride in history, which superseded any religious dogma. There was no need here for a private family mausoleum of the type being constructed elsewhere,[57] as the church adequately provided that function. The family controlled both estate and church, and provided an enduring commonality between the two.

## Conclusion

It is tempting to think of the increasingly monumentally congested church or chapel as symbolic of the entire families commemorated therein. Had the wheel turned full circle therefore? Did the meaning of such a chapel resonate in a medieval monument such as Bishop Stafford's, which although personalised for himself, was also, through the heraldry, intended to represent his wider family? The medieval monument was chiefly an artefact commissioned to encourage intercessory prayer for the soul of the departed and his family. The location of the monument was pivotal in encouraging such activity and a profitable mutuality between locus, imagery and liturgy was employed to maximal effect. The abandonment of the doctrine of Purgatory and the need for intercessory prayers necessitated a change in the meaning of post-Reformation monuments by which they became almost exclusively social tools, crucial in enhancing the family status and continuity of the dynasty at a time of a succession crisis. The imagery and locus of a monument remained critical, but liturgy was reduced to funeral ceremonies and the transitory effects of a funeral sermon. Far from just representing the dead, monuments were now reminiscent of the living and the didactic qualities of their virtuous lives, encouraging prayer not for the souls of the departed but for the well-being of the living. Monuments had become part of the social fabric, shifting from the emotionalism of the death of the commemorated to a celebration of the heroic virtuousness of their life, all combined with the concept of family *memoria*. Their liturgical context, however paramount prior to the Reformation, rapidly became superfluous thereafter, assuredly replaced by a family's sense of confidence, landed security, and eventually a complete belief in itself.

**Notes**

1  J. Weever, *Ancient Funerall Monuments* (1631), unpaginated 'Epistle to the reader'.

2  B. Kemp, *English Church Monuments* (1980).

3  B. Cherry, 'Some cathedral tombs', in M. Swanton (ed.), *Exeter Cathedral: A Celebration* (Exeter, 1991), 156–67.

4  E. F. Jacob (ed.), *The Register of Henry Chichele, Archbishop of Canterbury 1414–1443*, II (Oxford, 1938), 154.

5  N. Orme, 'The medieval chantries of Exeter cathedral – III', *Devon and Cornwall Notes and Queries [DCNQ]* 35 (1982), 67–71, (p. 68).

6  N. Orme, *Exeter Cathedral: The First Thousand Years, 400–1550* (Exeter, 2009), 67. I am most grateful to Professor Orme for discussing the Exeter bishops' tombs with me.

7  Orme, 'Medieval chantries', *DCNQ* 34 (1981), 319–26, (pp. 320–22).

8  A. M. Morganstern, *Gothic tombs of kinship* (Pennsylvania, 2000), passim, provides similar models for this rationale of intercessory recall.

9  D. Lepine and N. Orme (eds.), *Death and Memory in Medieval Exeter* (Exeter, 2003), 30–31.

10  Orme, *Exeter Cathedral*, 67.

11  W. Lack, H. M. Stuchfield and P. Whittemore, *The Monumental Brasses of Devonshire* (2000), 112, 116.

12. N. Rogers, '"Et expectis resurrectionem mortuorum": Images and texts relating to the Resurrection of the dead and the Last Judgement on English brasses and incised slabs', in N. Morgan (ed.), *Prophecy, Apocalypse and the Day of Doom* (Donington, 2004), 342–55, (p. 350).

13  F. C. Hingeston-Randolph, *The Register of Edmund Stafford* (1886), 404–05.

14  Langeton bequeathed 20s to John Wylle, chaplain, to pray for his soul, which sum, while not sufficient to maintain a chantry, would have ensured ceremonies of remembrance were enacted; see Hingeston-Randolph, *Stafford*, 405.

15  N. Orme, 'Sir John Speke and his chapel in Exeter Cathedral', *Transactions of the Devonshire Association* 118 (1986), 25–41.

16  F. W. Weaver (ed.), *Somerset Medieval Wills 1383–1500* (1901), 145, translation from the Latin original now The National Archives [TNA], PROB11/3/195, will proved 27 January 1439.

17  TNA, PROB11/5/223v, will proved 22 January 1469.

18  Lepine and Orme (eds.), *Death and Memory*, 239–40.

19  Weaver (ed.), *Somerset Medieval Wills*, 92.

20  N. Rogers, 'Hic Iacet…: the location of monuments in late medieval parish churches', in C. Burgess and E. Duffy (eds.), *The Parish in Late Medieval England* (Donington 2006), 261–81, (p. 264).

21  Weaver (ed.), *Somerset Medieval Wills*, 290.

22  R. Marks, *Image and Devotion in Late Medieval England* (Stroud, 2004), 173–81.

23  L. L. Duncan, *Testamenta Cantiana: West Kent* (1906), 26, 28, 31.

24  S. Badham, 'Status and Salvation: the design of medieval English brasses and incised slabs', *The Monumental Brass Society*, XV (1997), 412–65.

25  Rogers, 'Images and Texts', 346–7.

26  J. J. Howard (ed.), *The Visitation of Suffolke* 2 vols (1866), I, 166–70.

27  J. R. Greenwood, 'Wills and brasses: some conclusions from a Norfolk study', in J. Bertram (ed.), *Monumental Brasses as Art and History* (Stroud, 1996), 82–102.

28  R. Houlbrooke, *Death, Religion and the Family in England 1480–1750* (Oxford, 1998), 330–71.

29. Weever, *Ancient Funerall Monuments*, 52.

30  N. Llewellyn, 'Honour in life, death and in the memory: funeral monuments in early modern England', *Transactions of the Royal Historical Society*, 6th series, 6 (1996), 179–200.

31  C. J. M. Faunch, 'Church monuments and commemoration in Devon *c*.1530–*c*.1660', (doctoral thesis, University of Exeter, 1998), 398–403.

32  N. Llewellyn, *Funeral Monuments in post-Reformation England* (Cambridge, 2000), 373.

33  TNA, PROB11/68/269v–270r, will proved 30 June 1585.

34  N. Llewellyn, *The Art of Death* (1991), 100–29.

35 K. Fincham and N. Tyacke, *Altars Restored: The Changing Face of English Religious Worship, 1547–c.1700* (Oxford, 2007), 59.

36 S. Roffey, *Chantry Chapels and Medieval Strategies for the Afterlife* (Stroud, 2008), 167–76.

37 S. E. Lehmberg, *Cathedrals under Siege: Cathedrals in English Society, 1600–1700* (Exeter, 1996), 228.

38 Faunch, 'Church monuments', 413–18, 427–31.

39 C. Brooks, 'Exeter Cathedral', *Archaeological Journal Supplement* 147 (1990), 24–34.

40 V. Harding, 'Choices and changes: death, burial and the English Reformation' in D. Gaimster and R. Gilchrist (eds.), *The Archaeology of Reformation 1480–1580* (Leeds, 2003), 386–98.

41 F. G. Emmison, *Elizabethan Life: Essex Gentry's Wills* (Chelmsford, 1978), 242.

42 M. E. Allen (ed.), *Wills of the Archdeaconry of Suffolk 1620–1624* (Woodbridge, 1989), 306.

43 Emmison, *Elizabethan Life*, 114.

44 J. Finch, 'A reformation of meaning: commemoration and remembering the dead in the parish church, 1450–1640', in Gaimster and Gilchrist (eds.), *Archaeology of Reformation*, 437–49, (pp. 442–7).

45 J. Guillim, *A Display of Heraldry: The Sixth Edition* (1724), 8–9.

46 N. Cuddy, 'Dynasty and display: politics and painting in England', in K. Hearn (ed.), *Dynasties: Painting in Tudor and Jacobean England 1530–1630* (1995), 11–20.

47 R. Tittler, *The Face of the City: Civic Portraiture and Civic Identity in Early Modern England* (Manchester, 2007).

48 J. Scodel, T*he English Poetic Epitaph: Commemoration and Conflict from Jonson to Wordsworth* (Ithaca and London, 1991), 277–311.

49 M. Baker, *Figured in Marble: The Making and Viewing of Eighteenth-Century Sculpture* (2000), 50–60.

50 D. Bindman and M. Baker, *Roubiliac and the Eighteenth-Century Monument: Sculpture as Theatre* (New Haven and London, 1995), 134–41.

51 C.S. Gilbert, *Historical and Topographical Survey of the County of Cornwall* 2 vols (Plymouth Dock, 1817–20), II, 832.

52 J. Whetter, *Cornish People in the 18th Century* (Gorran, 2000), 102–03.

53 M. Craske, *The Silent Rhetoric of the Body: A History of Monumental Sculpture and Commemorative Art in England, 1720–1770* (New Haven and London, 2007), 27.

54 P. Cockerham, *Continuity and Change: Memorialisation and the Cornish Funeral Monument Industry 1497–1660* (Oxford, 2006), 95.

55 Gilbert, *Cornwall*, II, 833.

56 M. I. Webb, *Michael Rysbrack, Sculptor* (1954), 183.

57 H. Colvin, *Architecture and the After-Life* (New Haven and London 1991), 283–326.

# Abused, neglected and forgotten: the story of the medieval cross slab

*Brian and Moira Gittos*

*Brian and Moira Gittos, founder members of the Church Monuments Society, have been studying medieval church monuments since the 1970s and have published widely on the subject.*

## Introduction

THE LITERATURE on medieval church monuments is skewed towards those with the highest visual impact and the most significant genealogical associations. Considerations of high status tombs, sculptured effigies and monumental brasses predominate, with other classes such as cross slab grave stones often ignored. They are, for instance, only rarely mentioned in Pevsner's *The Buildings of England* series, even when they are the oldest objects in the church. Our purpose is to demonstrate their importance and raise awareness of the contribution they make to our understanding of the past. Cross slabs were once the first choice of the higher echelons of society and since their use subsequently permeated down the social strata, they achieved a degree of longevity and continuity unparalleled by any other form of commemoration except headstones.[1] They reflect centuries of changing tastes and a wide spectrum of personal wealth, ranging from great artistic achievement utilising costly materials and sumptuous decoration down to locally-made products. But all tell of the world and society that created them.

So what do we mean by 'cross slab'? The term is surprisingly hard to define and it is difficult to justify excluding clearly related monuments simply because they transgress an arbitrary boundary. However, here 'cross slab' is taken to embrace commemorative monuments produced from a single stone and which usually have some form of cross as the principal decoration. Primarily a class intended to be recumbent, most of the medieval examples would have been a coffin lid or covered a grave. They can be tapered or rectangular with squared or shaped ends. Most show a cross head atop a shaft firmly planted on a base (Fig. 1) but each element is subject to many interpretations. Few head designs are identical with games being played, for instance, on the setting; the shape and number of the arms; the form of the terminals and any decoration at the centre. Bases may be stepped, arched, foliate or absent. The decoration may take many forms, such as incising, relief carving, inlay, painting or any combination. A slab at Wycliffe, Yorkshire employs relief carving, incising and separate letter inlays of lead (Fig. 2). Inevitably there is overlap with sculptured effigies, ledger slabs, incised slabs and monumental brasses, particularly when different decorative techniques are used together.

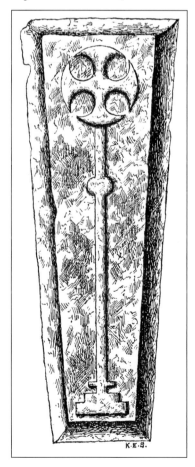

*Fig. 1: Cross slab of Stephen Langton, Archbishop of Canterbury 1206–28, at Canterbury Cathedral. The slab shows the archetypal arrangement of a cross on a tall shaft, standing on a stepped calvary. This design may be derived from processional crosses. From Styan, Sepulchral Cross-Slabs, Plate L.*

Fig. 2: *Fourteenth-century cross slab built into the south wall of the nave at Wycliffe, Yorkshire with incised cross, low relief head and inscription inlaid in lead. The shears are partly incised and partly bas-relief as though unfinished. Photo: B. & M. Gittos*

Fig. 3: *Cross slab in the cemetery of the church in the colonnaded street, Lepcis Magna, Libya. It can only have been laid down between the sixth and the tenth century. The slab has pendant alpha and omega and a Greek inscription on the cross. Photo: B. & M. Gittos*

## Origins

The origins of the cross slab can be traced, ultimately, to the gabled lids of classical sarcophagi. Common across the Romanised world, they continued into the Christian era with appropriate symbols added. Over time, their shape gradually flattened and crosses were marked out on the top, the ridge becoming the shaft. Several sarcophagi in York show a significant stage in this process. Used to denote Christian burials from early times, the cross could be viewed as protection for the deceased and an evocation of the burial rites for the living.

Cross slabs occur throughout Europe and are known from north Africa (e.g. Libya, Fig. 3) but are less frequent in the eastern Mediterranean with only isolated examples known from Greece.[2] The exception to this declining eastward trend is the kingdom of Armenia. Amongst many thousands of upright cross inscribed stones (khatchkars), carved body stones and recumbent figural incised slabs, some bear pastoral staffs (Fig. 4). Nearer to home, cross slabs were especially popular in Merovingian Gaul. The region around Poitiers abounds with examples, clearly derived from the lids of Roman sarcophagi. The Civaux cemetery is estimated to have contained 15,000 stone coffins and sufficient lids remain for a selection, placed upright, to form a bizarre churchyard wall (Fig. 5).[3] The Société Des Antiquaires de l'Ouest, based in Poitiers, collected some of the most elaborate examples (Fig. 6), which are now displayed in the Baptistère Saint-Jean.

Anglo-Saxon England produced a large number of cross slabs, with the symmetrical double-ended cross patterns being a common feature (Fig. 7), seemingly reflecting those of western France but more likely due to a common source in Roman tombs. Pre-conquest slabs survive in greatest numbers from the end of the period but examples can be found throughout the volumes of the Corpus of Anglo-Saxon Stone Sculpture. The Scandinavian-inspired monuments of the north and east, although typified by hogbacks, also included cross slabs using Viking decoration. Such individuality is also found in Scotland, Wales and Ireland. The large collection of cross inscribed memorials at Clonmacnois, Republic of Ireland,[4] for example, has a close affinity with other Irish art forms such as the high crosses, illuminated manuscripts and fine metalwork (Fig. 8). The monuments reflect the environment in which they were created.

## The golden age of cross slabs

The introduction of Norman culture is visible in the form and decoration of twelfth-century English cross slabs. Some have

*Fig. 4: Medieval inscribed body stones and khatchkars in the vast cemetery of Noraduz, Armenia. Photo: B. & M. Gittos*

*Fig. 5: Cross slabs and other coffin-shaped grave-markers, used to construct the boundary wall of the Merovingian cemetery at Civaux, Vienne, France. Photo: B. & M. Gittos*

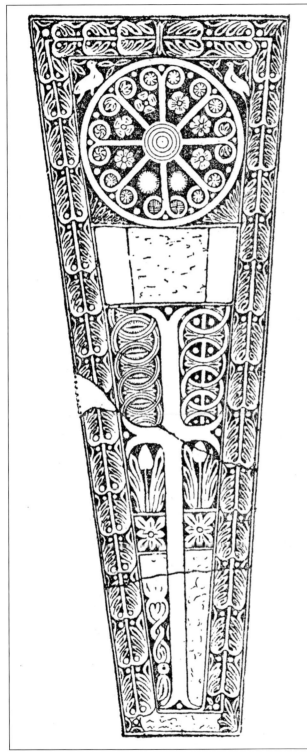

*Fig. 6 (left): Medieval cross slab from Antigny, now housed with other slabs in the Baptistery of St-Jean, Poitiers, France. From E. Ginot,* Le Baptistière Saint-Jean de Poitiers *(Poitiers, undated), catalogue no. 46.*

*Fig. 7 (right): Anglo-Saxon cross slab with crosses at both ends and interlace, found during excavations on the site of Cambridge Castle. From Boutell,* Christian Monuments, *15.*

*Fig. 8: Cross-inscribed grave slab to 'Suibine mac Mailae Humai', scribe of Clonmacnois, now lost. From a drawing by Petrie, in Macalister,* Memorial Slabs of Clonmacnois, *97.*

geometric patterns (Fig. 9) akin to those used architecturally, and the coffin-shaped slab becomes the norm. Throughout the following century, large numbers of cross slabs were produced in this country and they attained the apogee of their popularity. Demand continued through the Middle Ages and beyond but by the advent of the fourteenth century their pre-eminence had been usurped by other products, notably sculptured effigies and monumental brasses.

Slabs from this 'golden age' vary greatly in design, particularly the representation of the cross, selection of other decorative features and their arrangement. Most surviving examples are anonymous with only a small proportion identifiable through inscriptions or heraldry. However, the use of architectural and contemporary artistic features may give dating clues. In this regard, the popularity of leaves in cross head designs and branching from the shaft are especially useful. Stiff leaf appeared as early as the late twelfth century at Wells Cathedral and became a hallmark of the Early English style through the next century until discarded in favour of naturalistic representations prior to 1300. Early in the fourteenth century, naturalistic leaves gave way to more exuberant bulbous forms with the advent of the Decorated style.

*Fig. 9: Romanesque cross slab showing zig-zag patterning related to architectural motifs. Holy Trinity, Bradford-on-Avon, Wiltshire, churchyard. Photo: B. & M. Gittos*

This progression is reflected in the design of cross slabs and consequently some of the most striking and artistically successful examples date from the first half of the fourteenth century. Amongst a notable collection of slabs in the monk's dormitory at Valle Crucis Abbey (Clwyd) is one to Madog ap Gruffydd (d.1306).[5] He was the great-grandson of the abbey's founder and his fine monument (Fig. 10) was appropriately laid before the high altar. Vine stems with naturalistic leaves flank the centrally placed spear; the deceased is identified by the heraldry and the shield's border inscription. As well as demonstrating the use of contemporary leaf forms, the slab also highlights the difficulty of defining the term 'cross slab', as no actual cross is shown (except, perhaps, the shapes formed by the weapons). However, it fulfils the same function as a cross slab and is a closely related form. The remainder of this paper will consider in more detail the cross slabs to be found for the most part in English churches.

## Cross slab studies

The impression, given in the Introduction, of cross slabs being largely ignored is true in comparison to other forms of monument but they have attracted the attention of several antiquaries stretching back to Richard Gough in the late eighteenth century, who included four pages of slab drawings in his seminal work.[6] In 1849 the Revd Edward Cutts produced a manual on the subject, commenting in the preface 'This branch of archaeology has been hitherto much neglected, although it is a very interesting one and the examples are much more numerous than is generally imagined ...'.[7] More than a century and a half later this remains the standard work. Another useful contribution was made by Charles Boutell in 1854, illustrating and describing a large number of slabs.[8] Brindley and Weatherley (1887) ranged widely across the monument spectrum but included many well-illustrated cross slabs (Fig. 11).[9] K. E. Styan's 64 examples were drawn largely from the south and east of England and Wales.[10]

Since then writers have tended to treat cross slabs on an individual or regional basis. Canon Bower published a series of articles on the slabs in the Diocese of Carlisle, just prior to the second world war and Lawrence Butler's ground-breaking 1964 study dealt specifically with the East Midlands.[11] In the last 25 years a number of extremely thorough surveys of northern counties have been produced by Peter Ryder.[12] His most recent book, published in 2005, deals with Cumbria and is, like all his earlier works, fully illustrated with his own meticulously accurate drawings, which help to make them invaluable reference sources.[13] There are some less comprehensive county surveys such as the present authors' work on the East Riding of Yorkshire, Miller Christy on Essex and Ruth Butler and Leslie Jones' paper on Gloucestershire.[14] However, most English counties have yet to be surveyed and there is no country-wide bibliography.

The recent survey of Purbeck marble coffin-shaped slabs is described below and the pre-conquest survivals from England are

*Fig. 10 (left): Cross slab of Madog ap Gruffydd (d.1306), Vale Crucis Abbey, Clwyd. Photo: B. & M. Gittos*

*Fig. 11 (right): Late thirteenth-century slab in Brecon Cathedral. From Brindley & Weatherley,* Ancient Sepulchral Monuments, *plate 105.*

*Fig. 12: Fourteenth-century cross slab re-used in the north nave wall, Riccall, Yorkshire. Photo: B. & M. Gittos*

included in the emerging volumes of the Corpus of Anglo-Saxon Stone Sculpture, with a companion project underway in Wales. The growth of systematic church archaeology has begun providing more securely dateable evidence, although even when published, the material is scattered through the literature, buried in site reports.

## How many slabs?

The total number of English medieval cross slabs originally commissioned will never be known and it is only possible to make crude estimates. Very few slabs are in situ and those that remain are frequently incomplete, broken and damaged. Ironically, very many survive only because they were recycled as building material. Sometimes the pieces are still visible, for example on the stair turret of St Cuthbert's in Wells, Somerset; built into the tower and chancel walls at Kirby Grindalythe; or incorporated into the buttresses and exterior wall of the north aisle at Riccall (Fig. 12) (both Yorkshire). More often they are invisible, buried within the structure and found only during repairs or demolition.

When the nineteenth-century restorers at Bakewell, Derbyshire dismantled the tower, both transepts and the Vernon Chapel, they discovered numerous medieval grave slabs and crosses, in the foundations and walls.[15] Most were re-used (again!) in the new work but about 70 stones were retained and displayed. The total found was not recorded but contemporary sources suggest it could have been as high as 350. More recently, when the church of St Brandon, Brancepeth, County Durham was severely damaged by fire in 1998, the subsequent rebuilding programme revealed more than 70 medieval cross slabs. They had been incorporated into the walls, with many laid complete rather than broken up for rubble. During the large scale church restorations of the nineteenth century, many other similar but often unrecorded discoveries were made, which can be inferred from the collections of medieval slabs left behind. During the major 1864 restoration at Gainford, County Durham, some pre-conquest stones were uncovered which eventually joined the collection in Durham Cathedral library.[16] However, 27 cross slabs are still to be seen built into the walls and benches of the nineteenth-century porch with another standing inside. They were presumably revealed at the same time but there are no details of their discovery.

When the source is an historical description rather than archaeology, the monument type is rarely specified. For example, we know from surviving records of the large numbers of wealthy patrons who were buried in the lost monastic churches of London (such as the Black Friars) but can only surmise from considerations such as dates of death that many of these monuments were probably cross slabs.[17] Weever said of Christchurch (Aldgate) Priory in 1631: 'and seven score grave-stones of marble in divers places; all which were pulled downe, taken away, and sold for fiftie pounds or thereabouts, by *Sir Martin Bowes* Maior of London, An.1545'.[18] This is an extreme but not untypical story.

There is abundant evidence, therefore, of the wholesale destruction of medieval monuments country-wide particularly as a result of the Reformation. The cross slab was especially vulnerable because, once broken into pieces, it was ideal building material. Peter Ryder has suggested that the survival rate 'is probably less than 10% (and perhaps as little as 2-3%)'.[19] We fully support this suggestion but it could only be used to estimate the original total if the number of survivors were known. As an indication, Ryder lists 570 slabs in County Durham; 350 in South Yorkshire and about 450 in Cumbria. These figures are somewhat inflated by the inclusion of head stone, grave markers and a few known only from antiquarian drawings. However, our own researches have produced similar county totals elsewhere such as *c*.200 for the East Riding of Yorkshire and 141 for Dorset, to which should be added the results of the Purbeck marble coffin-shaped slab survey described below. Country-wide the total must, therefore, run to several thousands, almost certainly exceeding the more than five thousand surviving monumental brasses.

## Purbeck marble cross slabs

From 1994 to 2003, a survey of Purbeck marble coffin-shaped slabs was serialised in the *Church Monuments Society Newsletter*.[20] This listed all known examples, county by county, with members contributing further discoveries during the publication process. The objective was to compile a corpus of a category of monument which lasted from the later twelfth century into the fourteenth. They were initially highly prestigious but were subsequently supplied to less wealthy clients with production spanning the 'golden age' of cross slabs. We considered that a better understanding of high quality slabs would inform the study of these monuments as a whole. Many unexpected facts emerged, with the total count surprisingly as high as 820 and more still being recorded. There was strong evidence for primary transportation by water along the coast from Dorset and inland using navigable rivers. The contrast between Dorset with 100 slabs and the neighbouring county of Somerset with only eight makes the point well and also demonstrates that the sea journey around Lands End acted as a significant barrier. Travelling east, much further away in Yorkshire, there were more than twice as many slabs as Somerset. It was most surprising that many more survive in Norfolk than any other county.

Standard workshop products predominated, with the most common combination being double-hollow chamfered edges, cross botonnée head and three-step calvary (shown with the addition of trumpets and an inscription in Figure 13). However, there were also many highly individual commissions, which demonstrated how the marblers were also prepared to satisfy individual customers. Good examples are at Hampstead Norris, Berkshire (Fig. 14), where a mounted knight holds a war-like pose above a shield and Brent Pelham, Hertfordshire. The latter depicts an angel carrying the praying soul of the deceased, surrounded by evangelistic symbols, above a foliated cross, with its stem gripped by the teeth of a wyvern. Here is drama indeed and a unique composition. These are some preliminary observations but a full analysis of this survey is still to come.

## Regional styles

As with Purbeck marble slabs, stylistic groups using other stones can be distinguished throughout the country which show characteristic features of the workshops which produced them. Some are limited to a couple of similar slabs in the same church, such as a pair built into the nave wall benches at Patrington in Holderness, Yorkshire. Others can be found largely within a county, like the slabs with elaborate foliated cross heads in Herefordshire (Fig. 15). Products of the workshops at Barnack, Northamptonshire, which typically have double-omega shaped ribbons on the stem (Fig. 16), are distributed throughout the eastern counties from Lincolnshire to North Kent. Many, more local, groupings can be recognised. Examples include those with very distinctive cross heads of the twelfth and thirteenth centuries

*Fig. 13: Purbeck marble slab now in the Museum of London but found on the site of the Guildhall chapel. The most common form of Purbeck cross design is here flanked by trumpets, and the inscription commemorates Godfrey le Troumpour. From Boutell,* Christian Monuments, *100.*

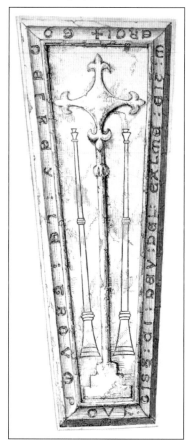

*Fig. 14: Thirteenth-century bas-relief figure of a charging knight, reminiscent of contemporary seal designs, from the Purbeck marble slab at Hampstead Norris, Berkshire. Photo: B. & M. Gittos*

around Cirencester; a collection of fifteenth/sixteenth century Ham Hill stone slabs in south Somerset and a series in and around Brecon, South Wales which continue into the post medieval period.

The use of symbols to indicate the deceased's profession or status shows a trend which cuts across many regional groupings. Such slabs bearing swords, shears (Fig. 17), chalices, books etc are most commonly found in the north and become progressively rarer further south. Amongst Purbeck marble slabs that at Morden, Dorset with six shields beside the cross stem is an exception, whereas Peter Ryder has shown how common symbols are in northern counties.

## The Gothic Revival and after
As well as having a dramatic effect on nineteenth-century church building and rebuilding, the Gothic Revival also created a

Fig. 15: Head of the cross from a fourteenth-century slab at Kingstone, Herefordshire. An example of the local style at this time, it also shows how designs can be drawn from other art forms, in this case, metalwork.
Photo: B. & M. Gittos

corresponding interest in medieval monuments, and cross slabs enjoyed a period of considerable popularity as many British churchyards testify. This continued into the twentieth century and the need for suitable designs was largely satisfied by the pattern books of monumental masons. However, genuine medieval monuments were also copied as can be seen with some memorials in the Camery cemetery of Wells Cathedral. Two medieval slabs which were then in the Chapter House crypt were copied to a high standard. One was used as a model for the monument of Walter Farrer, Archdeacon of Wells (d.1934) and the original is now mounted against the south wall of the cloister (Fig. 18). The second was copied for three memorials, to Eleanor Freeman (d.1902), widow of the historian Edward Freeman; Florence Cronshaw (d.1925) and another with a partly illegible inscription but also dated 1902.[21] Unfortunately, the second medieval slab has disappeared and, although it is also known from three nineteenth-century drawings, its loss means that the copies have become important records. At Piddlehinton, Dorset the memorial to Colonel John Dalrymple Belgrave (d.1955) imitates a Purbeck marble cross slab, with double hollow chamfered edges, four circle head, bar knop and three-step calvary. Inside the church porch rests a genuine Purbeck marble slab, which is worn and broken but probably provided the inspiration. An even more modern cross slab memorial is at Sutton Bingham, Somerset. George Aitken was headmaster of East Coker village school and an amateur archaeologist. He died in 1985 and his grave stone is a slightly coped slab bearing a relief cross with trefoil terminals and similar base.

## Vulnerability

The destruction of cross slabs has occurred throughout their history and unfortunately the process continues. What was done historically, for reasons of religious zeal and a lack of respect for memorials of the dead, is still happening, due to ignorance, plausible excuses and even considerations of heath and safety. A disturbing example of the latter occurred in Bristol in 1985. An interesting group of broken slabs lay in the churchyard of St Mary Redcliffe. We had previously noted them and arrived in the June to make an up-to-date detailed record. However, only a few of the larger pieces were still evident and enquiries eventually elicited a sorry story. Concerned that loose stones might be used by vandals to smash floodlights, the churchwardens offered the slabs to Bristol Museum, which declined as it was said they were of no particular importance. The church proceeded, therefore, to dispose of the monuments by smashing them with hammers and depositing the debris in a skip, which was taken to a landfill site near Bristol Airport where they were buried under thousands of tons of the City's rubbish. This case of modern vandalism is believed to have accounted for (amongst others) the greater part of a cross slab with incised Lombardic inscription, which Paul identified as commemorating a fourteenth-century carpenter, John Rowberwe (Fig. 19).[22]

Repairs to the tower at Rillington, Yorkshire in 1978 necessitated the replacement of the masonry of one of the buttresses. Amongst the displaced stones we noted eleven fragments of cross slabs and informed the vicar. Some of the pieces were still to be seen (in 2003) scattered in the grass beside the tower. Part of a Purbeck marble coffin-shaped slab served as a drain cover in the churchyard at Lytchett Matravers, Dorset in the 1990s but by 2000 it had disintegrated. The top half of another Purbeck marble cross slab used to lean against the exterior of the chancel east wall of All Saints, Dewlish, Dorset. In the mid 1990s a commemorative seat took its place and it was discarded. It was rediscovered underneath some bushes on the edge of the churchyard in 1999. English parish churches and churchyards are currently experiencing a period of considerable change and unidentified loose stones are clearly at high risk.

## Conclusions

Cross slabs are first and foremost memorials of the dead but they also have an important place in the country's cultural and artistic history. Some of the finest examples are objects of great beauty and they deserve special consideration. Unfortunately they are often mis-treated through ignorance of their importance and a national listing of cross slabs would provide a basis for ensuring

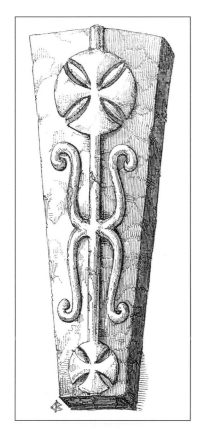

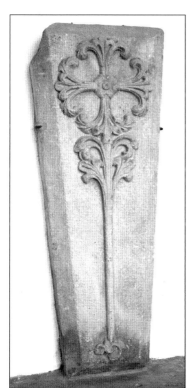

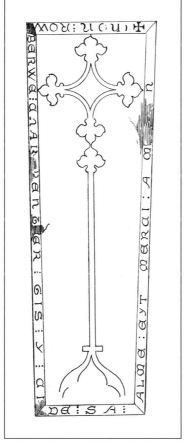

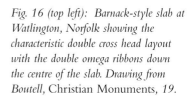

*Fig. 16 (top left): Barnack-style slab at Watlington, Norfolk showing the characteristic double cross head layout with the double omega ribbons down the centre of the slab. Drawing from Boutell, Christian Monuments, 19.*

*Fig. 17 (top right): Early fourteenth-century slab from Langtoft, East Yorkshire showing a representative bracelet head and with a Lombardic inscription commemorating Alina de Vale. Photo: B. & M. Gittos*

*Fig. 18 (bottom left): Thirteenth-century slab at Wells Cathedral (now in the cloister), copied in the early-twentieth-century. The design clearly derives its inspiration from contemporary metalwork.*
*Photo: B. & M. Gittos*

*Fig. 19 (bottom right): Fourteenth-century slab of John Rowberwe formerly at St Mary Redcliffe, Bristol. Most of this slab was disposed of in 1985. Drawing from Paul, Incised and Sepulchral Slabs, Plate II Fig. 1.*

their recognition and continued preservation. Recent important progress with cataloguing cross slabs in the north of England, provides a model for how this can be achieved but a great deal still needs to be done. We hope that this article will raise awareness of cross slabs and inspire others to take up their cause.

**Notes**

1   e.g. Alan, Abbot of Tewkesbury (d.1202); Stephen Langton, Archbishop of Canterbury (d.1228) and Godfrey Ludham, Archbishop of York (d.1265).

2   There are examples in the Byzantine Museum, Athens and the church of St Theodore, Mystras.

3   J.-P. Adam et al, 'Sud-Ouest et Centre', *Les Premiers Monuments Chrétiens de la France,* 2 (Paris, 1996), 273.

4   R. A. S. Macalister, *The Memorial Slabs of Clonmacnois, King's County* (Dublin, 1909).

5   C. A. Gresham, *Medieval Stone Carving in North Wales* (Cardiff, 1968), 137–40.

6   R. Gough, *Sepulchral Monuments of Great Britain,* 2 vols. (1786–99).

7   Revd E. L. Cutts, *A Manual for the Study of the Sepulchral Slabs and Crosses of The Middle Ages* (1849), v.

8   Revd C. Boutell, *Christian Monuments in England and Wales* (1854).

9   W. Brindley and W. S. Weatherley, *Ancient Sepulchral Monuments* (1887).

10  K. E. Styan, *A Short History of Sepulchral Cross-Slabs* (1902).

11  L. A. S. Butler, 'Minor medieval monumental sculpture in the East Midlands', *Archaeological Journal,* 121 (1964), 111–53.

12  P. Ryder, *The Medieval Cross Slab Grave Covers in County Durham,* Architectural and Archaeological Society of Durham and Northumberland, Research Report No.1 (Durham, 1985). P. Ryder, *Medieval Cross Slab Grave Covers in West Yorkshire* (Wakefield, 1991). P. Ryder, 'Medieval cross slab grave covers in Northumberland', *Archaeologia Aeliana,* Fifth Series, 28 (2000), 51–110; 30, (2002), 75–137; 32, (2003), 91–136.

13  P. Ryder, 'The medieval cross slab grave covers in Cumbria', *Cumberland and Westmorland Antiquarian and Archaeological Society,* Extra Series, 32 (Kendal, 2005).

14  B. and M. Gittos, 'A survey of East Riding sepulchral monuments before 1500', in C. Wilson (ed.), *Medieval Art and Architecture in the East Riding of Yorkshire,* The British Archaeological Association Conference Transactions for the Year 1983 (1989), 91–108. M. Christy, 'Some Essex coffin-slabs', *Transactions of the Essex Archaeological Society,* New Series, 7 (1900), 369–95. R. Butler & L. Jones, 'The cross-slabs of Gloucestershire', *Bristol and Gloucestershire Archaeological Society Transactions,* 91 (1972).

15  F. C. Plumptre, 'Some account of the parish church of Bakewell in Derbyshire and the early grave-stones and other remains discovered during the recent repairs', *Archaeological Journal,* 4 (1847), 37–58, (p. 47).

16  R. Cramp, (ed.), *County Durham and Northumberland,* Corpus of Anglo-Saxon Stone Sculpture in England, 1 part 1 (1984), 80.

17  A. W. Clapham, 'IV. On the topography of the Dominican Priory of London', *Archaeologia,* 63 (1912), 57–84, esp. 82–83.

18  J. Weever, *Ancient Funerall Monuments* (1631), 388.

19  Ryder, *West Yorkshire,* 5.

20  S. Badham, B. Gittos, M. Gittos and P. Lankester, 'Survey of Purbeck Marble coffin-shaped slabs', serialised in the *Church Monuments Society Newsletter,* in 15 parts, from 1994 (Vol. 10 No.1) to 2003 (Vol. 19 No. 1).

21  W. Rodwell, *Wells Cathedral: Excavations and Structural Studies* 1978–93, English Heritage Archaeological Report 21 (2001), 2, 493–94.

22  R. W. Paul, *An Account of Some of the Incised and Sepulchral Slabs of North-West Somersetshire* (1882), 1–2, Plate II Fig. 1.

# Deceptive appearances: the presentation of children on medieval tombs

*Sophie Oosterwijk*

IF THERE IS ONE AREA in the study of medieval monuments that has given rise to confusion and misinterpretation, it is that of child commemoration. Modern attitudes towards child death dictate that parents should love their children and mourn their loss, so any tomb figure resembling a child is likely to be regarded as a sign of parental affection, even if that 'child' looks rather like a miniature adult. On the other hand, some historians have taken the (presumed) absence of children on medieval monuments – or their inclusion as anonymous standardised clusters – as evidence that parents did not really feel child loss so very deeply. This essay will attempt to show how the truth about the appearance of children on medieval monuments is far more complicated than is often understood.

Dr Sophie Oosterwijk, FSA teaches art history at the University of St Andrews and is Hon. Editor of the journal Church Monuments.

## Weepers and joint monuments

Historians of childhood are apt to criticise the French historian Philippe Ariès, who in his book *Centuries of Childhood* proposed that childhood was 'discovered' only in the early modern period. He believed that, until the fourteenth century, medieval artists tended to depict children only as men on a reduced scale. In support of his argument, Ariès cited the evidence of monuments, claiming that children did not appear on tombs until the early sixteenth century, and that even then they were not portrayed on their own but represented first on their teachers' and then on their parents' monuments. The reason was obvious, in his opinion:

> No one thought of keeping a picture of a child if that child had either lived to grow to manhood or had died in infancy. In the first case, childhood was simply an unimportant phase of which there was no need to keep any record; in the second case, that of the dead child, it was thought that the little thing which had disappeared so soon in life was not worthy of remembrance: there were far too many children whose survival was problematical. The general feeling was, and for a long time remained, that one had several children in order to keep just a few.[1]

What Ariès failed to take into account was that 'realism' and 'portraiture' in the modern sense of the word were not the objective of medieval artists, and that there were other ways to remember or commemorate children besides effigies on tombs. The supposed absence of children on monuments – or of monuments to children – does not prove absence of affection, just as their

45

presence need not be evidence of affection. In fact, it was not just medieval children but also the majority of adults who ended up in anonymous graves and ultimately often (if burial space was limited) in charnel houses where their remains would be mingled with those of countless others. In the fourteenth-century Middle English poem *Pearl*, a Dreamer recounts how he 'felle vpon þat floury flaȝt' (fell upon that flowery stretch of turf ) to bemourn his dead daughter who lies buried there: 'I leste hyr in on erbere' (I lost her in an arbour).[2]

Ariès was not a medievalist and his use of art as historical evidence was both too literal and too much coloured by his own modern expectations of how a child should be depicted and

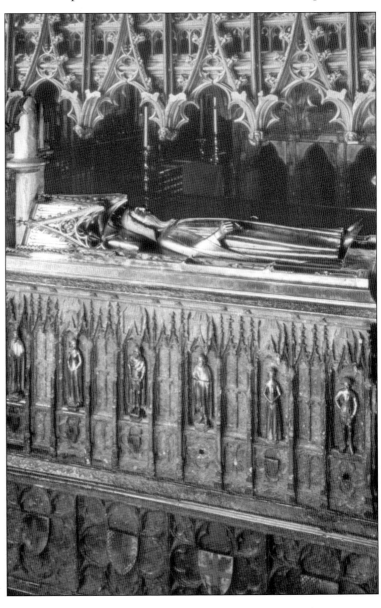

*Fig 1: Six surviving gilt-copper-alloy 'weepers' on the tomb chest of Edward III (d.1377) at Westminster Abbey: the figure on the far right probably represents the infant William of Windsor (d.1348). Photo: Dirk Visser*

treated. In his view, if medieval artists made children look like 'miniature adults' or 'men on a reduced scale', then this surely reflects how children were regarded in everyday life. Ariès' misconceptions about artistic conventions may help explain his failure to identify representations of children on medieval tombs, for he was wrong about their (virtual) non-appearance prior to the sixteenth century. Children appeared on medieval tombs in growing numbers from the late thirteenth century, when monuments changed from being the prerogative of royalty, aristocracy and the high clergy to becoming affordable also to the gentry and affluent middle-class burghers.

The most common appearance of children on medieval tomb is as so-called 'weepers', which are usually figures on the sides of tomb chests, although the term is here also applied to the rows of sons and daughters (or sometimes siblings) below the main effigies on brasses and incised slabs. An early example is the tomb chest of Edward III (d.1377) at Westminster Abbey, on which six of the originally twelve gilt-copper-alloy weepers remain, each representing one of the king's offspring (Fig. 1): their placement probably reflects the order of birth, which means that the figure on the far right represents William of Windsor, who died soon after birth in 1348.[3] Groups of 'weepers' on brasses are very rarely individualised and usually provide little or no indication about age, other than their respective sizes: even loose or covered hair on female figures may be simply convention rather than a sign of marital status.[4] The brass to Philipe Carrue (d.1414) in Beddington, Surrey, features a row of virtually identical siblings (Fig. 2), yet each figure is individually named and thus represents a person: the fact that four of the seven brothers are named John, two William, and two of the six sisters Agnes, suggests that some of these children were already dead but still remembered.

In fact, a crucial distinction should be made between 'children' and 'offspring' or 'siblings': weepers may be diminutive when compared to the main effigy of the deceased, perhaps because they were not the main focus of the monument, but even so they could represent adults. A good if highly unusual example is the curious fourteenth-century carved tomb slab of Sir John de Heslerton and his wife in Lowthorpe, Yorkshire, which features a family tree with branches terminating in the heads of the couple's thirteen offspring, with at least one son shown with a

*Fig. 2: Row of weepers on the brass of Philipe Carue (d.1414) at Beddington, Surrey. Rubbing: Martin Stuchfield*

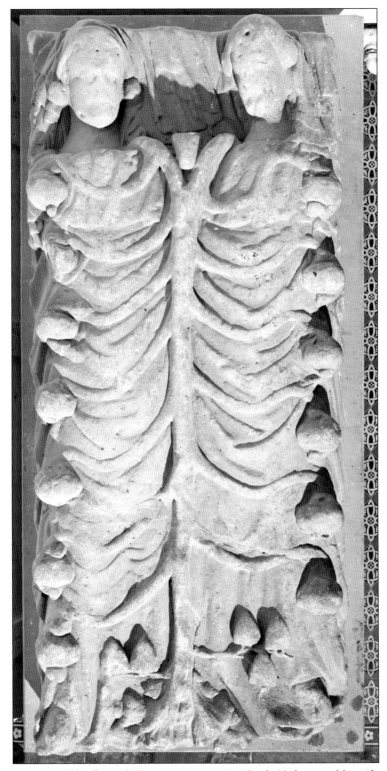

*Fig. 3: Double effigy probably commemorating Sir John de Heslerton and his wife, including the couple's children as heads on a family tree, mid fourteenth century, Lowthorpe, Yorkshire. Photo: C B Newham*

beard (Fig. 3). Likewise, although Edward III's weepers look like adults of different ages, three of his children had actually died in infancy and five others had also predeceased their father. One could thus argue that these weepers were more a dynastic statement than a commemoration of individual children, but they were included and thus remembered nonetheless.

It would appear that Ariès had a point in claiming that children appeared on their parents' tombs long before they were given their own memorials, albeit that they did not always appear just as conventional weepers. The recumbent effigy of Constantia at Scarcliffe in Derbyshire shows a mother holding her infant son John in a pose that is evidently derived from the more familiar standing Virgin and Child model, including the tender gesture of the child touching his mother's face with his hand (Fig. 4). As a

*Fig. 4: Tomb effigy of Constantia and her son John at Scarcliffe, Derbyshire, believed to be thirteenth-century. Photo: Sophie Oosterwijk*

provincial work this monument is difficult to date, and the deceased themselves have proved impossible to identify through records, but a thirteenth-century date cannot be ruled out. Another joint monument of the early fourteenth century is a worn effigial slab of a male civilian in South Anston church in Yorkshire (Fig. 5): the small female figure on the right probably represents the man's daughter, but their identities are unknown. Both figures are accompanied by angels: two are conventionally shown crouching on either side of the man's headrest while two others appear to be supporting the girl from above and below in a more unusual arrangement. These and other extant examples prove that children did occur on earlier medieval tombs.

## The 'miniature adult'

Even before the fourteenth century a few privileged children were honoured with their own monuments if not always effigies. In an article published in 1953, Joan Tanner mentioned among the earliest tombs of 'royal babies' in Edward the Confessor's chapel in Westminster Abbey, London, the two inlaid slabs of Margaret and John de Valence, who died in 1276 and 1277, respectively.[5] As their father William (d.1296) had married Joanna de Munchensi in 1247 and John was their eldest child, however, it seems improbable that John – and perhaps also Margaret – was still young enough to qualify as a 'child' in the modern sense of the word.

An earlier royal child burial in Westminster Abbey was that of Katherine, the beloved young daughter of Henry III and Eleanor of Provence. Chronicles tell us that she was very beautiful but of poor health.[6] When she died in 1257, not yet three-and-a-half years old, no expense was spared to commemorate the little girl. Her grief-stricken father originally planned a tomb with a gilt-copper-alloy effigy in her memory, but then changed his mind. Instead, he commissioned the royal goldsmith William of Gloucester to create an even more sumptuous silver image decorated with pearls and amethysts. Status and display were important to Henry, who was at the time engaged in rebuilding Westminster Abbey in what was clearly an attempt to emulate the commemorative programme at the royal abbey of Saint-Denis by his brother-in-law, Louis IX of France. However, dynastic concerns do not rule out genuine feeling behind the monument of a daughter whose loss left both parents virtually prostrate with grief.

Katherine's precious effigy has unfortunately failed to survive and we have no accurate description of its appearance or size. The fact that she was just a little girl does not mean that her tomb must have been an undersized one, for display was still a major

consideration. When Edward I's daughter Eleanor by his second wife Margaret of France died at the age of five in 1311, a huge inlaid slab measuring 120 x 45 in. was commissioned in her memory at Beaulieu Abbey by her half-brother Edward II.[7] The inlay has mostly been lost but the indent shows a female figure on a bracket – a feature that is not uncommon in combination with child effigies.[8]

Eleanor's brass slab was disproportionately large for a mere toddler, and a miniature effigy might seem much more appropriate in size for a child memorial. Yet appearances can again be deceptive. A particularly persistent fallacy is the sentimental myth of the so-called 'Stanley boy' effigy in Elford, Staffordshire, which is supposed to commemorate the last male Stanley heir killed by a tennis ball in or around 1460 (Fig. 6).[9] There is no historical evidence to support this identification and the story can only be traced back to the late sixteenth century. Moreover, a

curious discrepancy occurs in early accounts of the effigy: the Staffordshire antiquarian Sampson Erdeswicke (d.1603) described it as 'holding a ball to his ear', whereas according to Thomas Pennant in 1781 'one hand points to his ear; the other holds a ball'. These two varying descriptions may point to the true nature of this miniature effigy, which actually looks thirteenth-century in style, *i.e.* two centuries earlier than the Stanley heir it is supposed to commemorate and before that family was resident in Elford.

Miniature effigies were used to mark heart (and sometimes entrail) burials, an example being the pair of marble effigies of 1371–2 by Jean de Liège for King Charles IV the Fair (d.1328) and his wife Jeanne d'Evreux, who are shown holding a bag with their entrails (now Paris, Louvre). Two of the three miniature effigies in Berkeley church in Gloucestershire still hold broken objects that may represent their hearts, while in nearby Coberley a female miniature effigy of the early fourteenth century is shown inserting her right hand into her bodice (Fig. 7), thereby presumably indicating another heart burial.

The Elford effigy may originally have commemorated a similar heart burial with the 'ball' in the left hand representing the heart. Over time such miniature effigies were frequently mistaken for child monuments. Historical evidence and the overall

*Fig. 7: Early-fourteenth-century female miniature effigy, probably commemorating a member of the Berkeley family, at Coberley, Gloucestershire. Photo: C B Newham*

appearance of the Elford effigy suggest that this may be a post-medieval forgery created to replace a badly damaged thirteenth-century monument that had already attracted antiquarian interest. The 'Stanley boy' monument was restored yet further by Edward Richardson in 1848; the plinth with its dubious Latin motto *Ubi dolor ibi digitus* ('Where the pain is, there is the finger') is probably his work. A popular story thus may hide the truth about a less palatable medieval custom and this should serve as a warning against interpreting miniature effigies unquestioningly as child memorials.

## *Age and idealisation*

There is yet another confusing element in many medieval child memorials, and that is the evident discrepancy between the appearance of the effigy and the child's actual age. A good example is the weeper that is supposed to represent the infant William of Windsor (d.1348) on the tomb chest of his father Edward III (Fig. 1). Why would a dead baby be depicted as an idealised youth? Admittedly, a swaddled infant might not look very impressive on a royal monument. Yet this example is not unique: the small Purbeck marble tomb that William shares with his infant sister Blanche of the Tower (1340–42) at Westminster

Abbey features a double miniature effigy in alabaster that depicts them both as youngsters (Fig. 8). Whereas William is shown in a short tunic and tight hose, Blanche is presented as an elegant female with her hair tied up in fashionable cauls on either side of her face.[10] A similar age discrepancy is evident at York Minster in the monument to their brother William of Hatfield, who was born just before Christmas 1336 but died in early 1337; his alabaster effigy shows him as an elegantly dressed young prince (Fig. 9).[11] Yet medieval people recognised childhood as a specific stage of life; in fact, variations of the popular theme of the Ages of Man distinguish separate ages of infancy, boyhood and youth.[12] So if infancy was a recognised phase, why then are these three royal infants not commemorated as such?

*Fig. 8: Alabaster monument to William of Windsor (d. 1348) and Blanche of the Tower (d. 1342) at Westminster Abbey. Photo: University of Leicester*

*Fig. 9: Alabaster monument to Prince William of Hatfield (d. 1337) in York Minster. Photo: National Monuments Record*

The tomb representations of Edward III's infant offspring are not simply idealised images of those children as they might have been if only they had survived, as has sometimes been suggested. Instead the effigies may reflect medieval theological thinking about the perfect age of Christ that the blessed would attain in heaven. Theologians based this idea on St Paul's epistle to the Ephesians iv. 13 ('Until we all meet into the unity of faith, and of the knowledge of the Son of God, unto a perfect man, unto the measure of the age and of the fulness of Christ'); the words *in virum perfectum* were interpreted as a reference to Christ, who was traditionally believed to have died at the age of thirty-three.[13] Moreover, Christ's ideal female counterpart was the Virgin Mary, who was traditionally believed to have been either twelve or fifteen at the time of the Annunciation, and this fits in with the strong medieval cult of virginity.[14] The idea of the perfect age in heaven also underlies the poem *Pearl*, in which the Dreamer's dead infant daughter appears to him as a heavenly bride of Christ with divine wisdom to match.

Other known child memorials across Europe similarly depict the deceased as young adults instead of children, which may confuse the modern viewer no less than miniature effigies are likely to do. Just as William of Hatfield's alabaster effigy looks in no way like an infant, there is nothing child-like about the incised slab at St Bees Priory, Cumberland, of Joan de Lucy, who was not yet three years old when she died in 1369 (Fig. 10).[15] Joan is shown as a tall lady with her hair tied up in cauls, rather like Blanche of the Tower's slightly later alabaster effigy. While these effigies indicate the gender of the deceased, they give no indication of age.

The formal hairstyle on the effigies of Joan and Blanche is itself confusing because loose hair was traditionally a sign of virginity. Yet it would be incorrect to interpret female effigies with long loose hair as 'maidens', as is too often done. For example, medieval queens wore their hair untied at their coronation, and

*Fig. 10: 'Maidenly' incised slab of Joan de Lucy (d.1369) at St Bees Priory, Cumberland. Rubbing: F. A. Greenhill*

Eleanor of Castile (d.1290) is indeed portrayed thus both on her gilt-copper-alloy effigy and on the Eleanor Crosses that her widower Edward I erected in her memory.[16] The same 'virginal' hairstyle – sometimes in combination with a garland of flowers – can be found on memorials to married women, older spinsters, and young girls: a bewildering variety that makes it hazardous to draw conclusions about age or marital status in relation to 'maidenly effigies' that cannot be identified through an epitaph or reliable documentary evidence. The problem can be illustrated by two identifiable 'maidenly' brasses. The epitaph accompanying the brass of Cecilie Boleyn at Blickling in Norfolk states that she died on 26 June 1458 'in her maydenhode of the age of .l. [= 50] years', while Joan, Lady Cromwell (d.1490), who was twice married, is also depicted with long flowing locks on her magnificent brass in Tattershall, Lincolnshire. Yet there is no evidence whatsoever about age or status for Johane Plessi, whose half-effigy brass of *c*.1360 survives at Quainton, Buckinghamshire, or for the *c*.1450 brass to an unidentified garlanded lady at Lingfield, Surrey.[17] On the other hand, the fact that Margarete Brocas is shown alongside her brother Raulin on their joint half-effigy brass of *c*.1360 at Sherborne St John in Hampshire suggests that both died as children or unmarried adolescents.[18]

In short, just as medieval effigies to adults were usually idealised rather than true to life, the same applies to child effigies. In some cases, 'maidenly' effigies may have been intended to reflect a theological ideal, whereas other conventional tomb figures may simply have indicated nothing more than gender. Of course, we must remember that epitaphs and other identifying markers have all too often been lost over time, which can make it extremely hard to identify child memorials with any certainty: after all, appearances can be deceptive.

## Chrysoms

Yet by the end of the Middle Ages, idealisation had begun to make way for more true-to-life representations. One distinct later variety of child effigy is the so-called 'chrysom'; a term traditionally used for an effigy of a swaddled baby (Fig. 11). Although relatively little is known about swaddling – whether method, materials or duration – it had been customary since antiquity to wrap babies in tight cloths and bands after birth in order to keep them warm and ensure that their limbs would grow straight instead of crooked.[19] In England this custom was abandoned in the course of the eighteenth century, although it is still being practised in other parts of the world to this day.

'Chrysom' effigies started occurring on tombs during the fourteenth century, an example being the worn tomb slab of an unknown mother and baby in Welby, Lincolnshire, although it was only in the later fifteenth century that they became more common as independent memorials to infants. Hardly naturalistic in their appearance, these images would nonetheless have been immediately recognisable as babies to a medieval viewer. The term 'chrysom' is derived from the word 'chrism', *i.e.* the holy oil with

Fig. 11: 'Chrysom' brass of Elyn Bray (d.1516), Stoke D'Abernon, Surrey. Rubbing: Martin Stuchfield

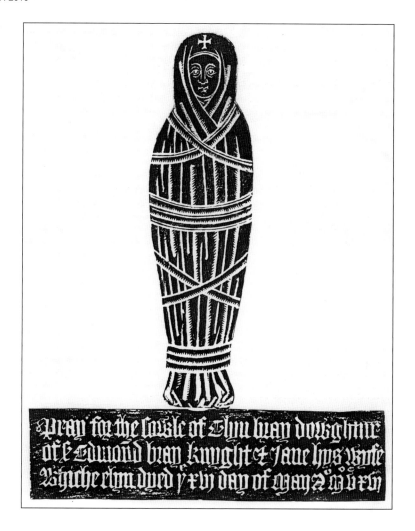

which babies were given the sign of the cross at baptism. This etymology may be the origin of a mistaken belief that 'chrysom' effigies are shown wearing their chrisom cloth to indicate that the commemorated child had died baptised but before the mother had been churched – a tradition that is still being perpetuated in more recent scholarship.[20] Yet according to the Oxford English Dictionary, the word 'chrisom' could mean both a baptismal cloth, and hence 'a child in its chrisom-cloth; a child in its first month; an innocent babe', who might also be called a 'chrisomer'. In other words, the meaning shifted from just the cloth to describe the child itself. We find a variation of the term 'chrisom child' in Shakespeare's *Henry V*, act II, scene iii, when the Hostess sums up Falstaff's demise: 'A made a finer end, and went away an it had been any christom child'. The implication is clear here: Falstaff died a good death, much like an innocent baby cleansed of original sin by baptism, and his soul's salvation cannot be in doubt.

The cross that marks some 'chrysom' effigies may indeed imply baptism, an example being the brass of Elyn Bray (d.1516) in Stoke d'Abernon, Surrey, where her name given in the epitaph proves that she died baptised. Nonetheless, these effigies indicate first and foremost death in early infancy, and as such they are more true to life than the earlier idealised representations of children as young adults.

## Conclusion

It will be clear from the above that Ariès was wrong in claiming that children were considered 'not worthy of remembrance' in the Middle Ages. Nevertheless, it cannot be denied that children only start appearing on monuments more frequently from the late thirteenth century onwards, and even then one has to search for examples; permanent child memorials with or without effigies were still unusual rather than the norm. Moreover, artists evidently had to invent ways of presenting children on tombs in line with patrons' expectations, artistic conventions and religious thinking of the period, resulting in a variety of depictions that are not always immediately recognisable as children to a modern viewer. What should be emphasised is that monuments are not proof of affection *per se*. Medieval children had little or no social status as such, and dead children are, to put it bluntly, ultimately a dynastic and biological failure. Child monuments and the inclusion of offspring as weepers may indeed often have been inspired by dynastic considerations, but this does not preclude the idea of affection for children and heartfelt grief at their loss. It is true that there was a very real risk of death at a very early age, and parents were aware of this. However, it would be wrong to assume that children were neither loved nor remembered. Even the anonymous rows of offspring on monuments suggest that every child counted.

## Acknowledgements

*I am grateful to Cameron Newham, Martin Stuchfield and Dirk Visser for their help in providing illustrations, and to Sally Badham for her valuable editorial input.*

**Notes**

1   P. Ariès, *Centuries of Childhood*, (1960, transl. 1962, repr. Harmondsworth, 1986), 36. Among medieval historians, criticising Ariès is regarded as flogging a dead horse, but his ideas have proved very tenacious. On the subject of the appearance of children on medieval monuments, see S. Oosterwijk, '"A swithe feire graue": the appearance of children on medieval tomb monuments', in R. Eales and S. Tyas (eds.), *Family and Dynasty in the Middle Ages*, (1997 Harlaxton Symposium Proceedings), Harlaxton Medieval Studies, 9, (Donington, 2003), 172–92.

2   E.V. Gordon (ed.), *Pearl*, (Oxford, 1963), lines 57, 9.

3   This is an example of a so-called 'kinship tomb', as discussed in A. McGee Morganstern, *Gothic Tombs of Kinship in France, the Low Countries and England*

(University Park, Pennsylvania, 2000), esp. 117–32 and fig. 75.

4   For further examples, see J. Page-Phillips, *Children on Brasses* (1970), e.g. the weepers from the brass of Thomas (d.1483) and Isabel Hampton in Stoke Charity, Hampshire in fig. 19, which do show subtle differences between the couple's six daughters.

5   J. D. Tanner, 'Tombs of royal babies in Westminster Abbey', *Journal of the British Archaeological Association*, 16, (1953), 25–40, at 31–32; S. Badham, 'Edward the Confessor's Chapel, Westminster Abbey: the origins of the royal mausoleum and its cosmatesque pavement', *The Antiquaries Journal*, 87, (2007), 197–219, esp. 201–06 and figs. 2–3.

6   Tanner, 'Tombs of royal babies', 26–28; M. A. E. Green, *Lives of the Princesses of England*, 6 vols., (1850), vol. 2, 270–74; M. Howell, 'The children of King Henry III and Eleanor of Provence', in P. R. Coss and S. D. Lloyd (eds.), *Thirteenth Century England*, vol. 4, Proceedings of the Newcastle upon Tyne Conference 1991, (Woodbridge, 1992), 57–72.

7   S. Badham and M. Norris, *Early Incised Slabs and Brasses from the London Marblers*, Reports of the Research Committee of the Society of Antiquaries of London No. 60, (1999), pp. 62–67.

8   Compare, for example, the children placed on brackets or pedestals on the Corp brass in Stoke Fleming, Devon, on the brasses of Sir Reginald Braybrooke and Sir Nicholas Hawberk at Cobham, Kent, and on the lost brass to Thomas of Woodstock in Westminster Abbey (as recorded in F. Sandford's *Genealogical History of the Kings and Queens of England* (1677), 230).

9   See Oosterwijk, 'A swithe feire graue', 190 and pl. 46; S. Oosterwijk, 'Of tombs and tales ...', *Church Monuments Society Newsletter* 22:2, (Winter 2006/7), 16–18.

10  See Oosterwijk, 'A swithe feire graue', 183–84 and pl. 43. The double effigy was not created until 1376 when Edward III ordered John Orchard to carry out some additional work on Queen Philippa's monument; see H. M. Colvin (ed.), *The History of the King's Works: The Middle Ages*, 3 vols., (1963), vol. 1, 486.

11  Sally Badham, 'Yorkshire's royal monument re-visited', *Church Monuments Society Newsletter*, 25:1, (Summer 2009), 12-15.

12  For the Ages of Man, see J. A. Burrow, *The Ages of Man: a Study in Medieval Writing and Thought* (1986, repr. Oxford, 1988); E. Sears, *The Ages of Man: Medieval Interpretations of the Life Cycle* (Princeton, 1986); M. E. Goodich, *From Birth to Old Age: the Human Life Cycle in Medieval Thought, 1250–1350* (1989); Deborah Youngs, *The Life-Cycle in Western Europe, c.1300–c.1600* (Manchester, 2006).

13  The idea of the perfect age is discussed in M. Twycross, '"With what body shall they come?" Black and white souls in the English mystery plays', in: H. Phillips (ed.), *Langland, the Mystics and the Medieval English Religious Tradition: Essays in Honour of S. S. Hussey* (Cambridge, 1990), 271–86; see also Oosterwijk, 'A swithe feire graue', esp. 181–82.

14  The literature on medieval maidens and virgin saints is vast. See, for example, A. Bernau, S. Salih and R. Evans (eds.), *Medieval Virginities, Religion & Culture in the Middle Ages* (Cardiff, 2003); K. M. Phillips, *Medieval Maidens: Young Women and Gender in England, 1270–1540* (Manchester, 2003).

15  F. A. Greenhill, *Incised Effigial Slabs: a Study of Engraved Stone Memorials in Latin Christendom, c.1100 to c.1700* (1976), vol. I, 241, and vol. II, fig. 138a.

16  See P. Lindley, 'Romanticizing reality: the sculptural memorials of Queen Eleanor and their context', in D. Parsons (ed.), *Eleanor of Castile 1290–1990: Essays to Commemorate the 700th Anniversary of her Death, 28 November 1290* (Stamford, 1991), 69–92.

17  For the brasses at Chenies and Quainton, see W. Lack, H. M. Stuchfield and P. Whittemore, *The Monumental Brasses of Buckinghamshire* (1994), 37–38 and 177–78; for the Lingfield brass, see N. Saul, *Death, Art, and Memory in Medieval England: the Cobham Family and their Monuments 1300–1500* (Oxford, 2001), 186 and fig. 33.

18  Page-Phillips, *Children on Brasses*, fig. 1.

19  See S. Oosterwijk, 'Chrysoms, shrouds and infants on English tomb monuments: a question of terminology?', *Church Monuments*, 15, (2000), 44–64.

20  N. Orme, *Medieval Children*, (New Haven/London, 2001), 102 (fig. 36), 120–21.

# What an epitaph can tell us: recovering the world of John Lovekyn

*Nigel Saul*

*Nigel Saul is Professor of Medieval History, Royal Holloway, University of London.*

A MODEST BRASS EPITAPH on the vestry wall of Walkern church, Hertfordshire, tells a story which connects three religious buildings – Walkern church itself, St Michael's, Crooked Lane in London, and the Lovekyn Chapel at Kingston upon Thames, Surrey. The brass is an example of a palimpsest – that is to say, of one which has been taken up and reused. On the obverse is an inscription to Richard, son of John Humberstone of Walkern, who died in 1581 (Fig. 1). On the reverse is part of an inscription, of which both ends have been trimmed. It commemorates a Londoner, John Lovekyn (d.1368), sometime mayor of the city of London. Lovekyn is known to have been buried in the church of St Michael, Crooked Lane, off Eastcheap, and his brass was originally laid there (Fig. 2).

The wording of the inscription to Lovekyn is of considerable interest. Not only does it shed light on the matter of his personal religion; it also assists in the understanding of his intentions regarding the other institution with which he was associated, the third of our buildings, the Lovekyn Chapel at Kingston upon Thames (Fig. 3). The inscription is composed of three Latin verses and reads:

> [Ve]rmibus esca datur Lovekyn caro pulcra [Johannis]
> [Bi]s fuit hic maior iterum bis Rege jube[nte]
> [A]nno milleno ter C cum septuageno

The lines may be translated as:

> The flesh of John Lovekyn is given, a fine food for worms
> Twice he was mayor here, twice again at the king's command
> One thousand three hundred and seventy

John Stow, the sixteenth-century London antiquary, tells us something of the background to Lovekyn's brass. In his *Survey of London* he records that Lovekyn was originally commemorated in St Michael's, Crooked Lane, 'in the quire, under a faire tombe, with the images of him and his wife in alabaster'. Lovekyn had substantially rebuilt St Michael's, originally a very small building. However, the fabric was 'increased' again (in Stow's words) 'with a new Quier and side chappels' by Lovekyn's apprentice, executor and eventual successor in his business, Sir William Walworth. At the same time as undertaking this work, Stow adds, Walworth removed Lovekyn's original tomb monument and replaced it with a marble slab bearing brasses.[1]

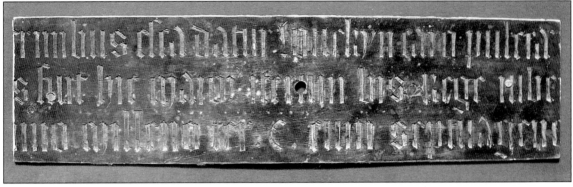

*Fig. 1 (top): Brass inscription from Walkern, Hertfordshire to Richard, son of John Humberstone of Walkern (d. 1581).*
*Fig. 2 (bottom): Palimpsest reverse of brass to Richard Humberstone, showing inscription to John Lovekyn (d. 1368). Both photos: H. M. Stuchfield*

Stow's account presents problems of interpretation, as the removal of a tomb of relatively recent date seems an extraordinarily high-handed action for Walworth to have taken. One possible way of understanding the text is to suppose that Walworth did indeed replace the monument with a brass, prompted perhaps by the need to free up processional routes in the church. Another possibility, however, is to suppose that Stow misunderstood what happened, and that Walworth, instead of replacing the tomb, simply supplemented it with a brass epitaph, perhaps over Lovekyn's actual burial place. Whichever interpretation is favoured, there can be little doubt about one thing: that the brass to Lovekyn was laid some years after his death. Confirmation of this is found in one feature otherwise difficult to explain: that the date given for Lovekyn's death is incorrect. Lovekyn is said to have died in 1370, whereas in fact he died in 1368. Such an error is only explicable on the assumption that the inscription was commissioned some time after Lovekyn's passing, when memories were fading. Walworth, the man who was to win notoriety for the killing of Wat Tyler in the Great Revolt, lived until early 1386. Quite possibly the laying of the epitaph was a project of his later years, as he began to think about his own commemoration. The evidence of the epigraphy of the epitaph would be consistent with a date in the early 1380s.

The removal of the brass from St Michael's, Crooked Lane, probably took place in Edward VI's reign, when, as Stow tells us, Walworth's own monument was severely defaced by what he called 'bad people'. There can be little doubt that Lovekyn's brass was gone by 1562, for in that year the Fishmongers' Company undertook restorations to both monuments, in the case of Lovekyn's providing an entirely new inscription. The brass's removal and recycling were paradoxically to prove its salvation. St Michael's, Crooked Lane, was completely destroyed in the Great Fire and had to be rebuilt from the foundations. Nothing else of its contents is known to have survived. The rebuilt church was in its turn demolished in the mid nineteenth century, and the site is now occupied by offices and an enlarged traffic junction.

St Michael's, Crooked Lane, was very much the Fishmongers' church in the late Middle Ages. Lovekyn was a leading fishmonger and his house a little to the south of the church, off what is now Upper Thames Street, is today the Fishmongers Hall. Lovekyn had been a man of great wealth and consequence in London in the mid fourteenth century. He carried on an extensive business in salted or stockfish, corn, wheat, oats, beans, herrings and sea coal, and he traded extensively abroad. He was one of London's two aldermanic representatives in parliament in 1344, 1346, 1348 and 1365. He served four times as Lord Mayor of London, in 1348, 1358, 1365 and 1366. He owed the third of his mayoral appointments directly to the king, who installed him in the place of Adam Bury, despite the fact that the latter had been re-elected after serving as mayor in the previous year. Lovekyn evidently valued the high standing which he enjoyed in royal favour: he made sure that his executors knew about it, and mention was made of the fact on his epitaph.

Lovekyn was a second generation Londoner. He was either the son or the nephew of Edward Lovekyn, a native of Kingston upon Thames, who had himself built up a substantial fortune and acquired the citizenry of London. Whereas the younger Lovekyn's interests were centred almost wholly in the capital, those of his father appear to have been equally divided between his home town and his adopted city. In 1309 Edward Lovekyn had set aside property in Kingston to found a chantry chapel for the benefit of his soul and the souls of all the faithful departed. This was the chantry chapel dedicated to St Mary Magdalene, for which he provided a site just beyond the eastern end of the town on what is now London Road.[2] The chantry enjoyed a rather chequered existence in its first half century, and in the wake of the Black

Death, when the tenements which were the main source of its income stood empty, it was badly decayed. In 1352 John Lovekyn, in a gesture of dynastic piety, re-founded the chapel. He provided it with new lands, in both Kingston and London, to support an additional chaplain, and he completely rebuilt the fabric. His chapel survives today and is a rare example of a complete ecclesiastical building of the 1350s.

The ordinances which Lovekyn provided for his chantry provide a fascinating insight into his thinking on matters of institutional religion. They reveal him as a preoccupied with regulation and control. He sought to provide for every aspect of his chaplains' lives.[3] They were to swear immediately on institution to reside continuously at the chapel; they were to minister personally at the chapel and not to engage in any service elsewhere; the income of the chapel was to be applied for the benefit of the chapel and in no other way; the chaplains were to have their meals together in the same apartment and each sleep in his own chamber; the warden was to provide a competent clerk to serve at mass and to minister to the chaplains in their chambers; the warden was to supply the chaplains with comely surplices and amices trimmed with black fur; none of the chaplains except the warden was to introduce a stranger at the expense of the house; the warden and chaplains were entirely to abstain from taverns, and the latter should not visit any house without the warden's leave. Further regulations were made for the various daily services, which were to be after the Use of Sarum; and the details of these services were then given.

The thinking behind Lovekyn's ordinances is very clear. He was determined to ensure no dereliction of duty on the chaplains' part in the provision of intercession for his and the other beneficiaries' souls. The safe passage of the souls of these people was entirely dependent on the chaplains' good standing with the Almighty. And because of this, he was anxious to ensure the chaplains' purity of life: any moral lapse would weaken the value of their prayers and compromise the safety of men's souls. Most people in the Middle Ages approaching the end of their earthly days were concerned with their safe passage in the afterlife, and most who could afford it provided for priestly intercession. John Lovekyn's concern, while conventional enough, appears to have bordered on the obsessive. His chapel at Kingston may not have been the only intercessory foundation he established. If Leland is to be believed, he also founded a college of priests at St Michael's, Crooked Lane.[4]

In the light of this evidence of Lovekyn's religious beliefs we can now return to the epitaph on his brass at Walkern. The epitaph hints at an aspect of his piety which accords quite closely with the

*Fig. 3: The Lovekyn Chapel at Kingston upon Thames, Surrey. Photo: N. Saul*

mood revealed by the ordinances; that is its austerity, its concern with personal self-abasement. In the opening line of the epitaph Lovekyn speaks with feeling of his contempt for the flesh: 'John Lovekyn, fine food for worms'. Lovekyn is shown recognising the transience of human life. Proud and rich as he is in this world, he accepts that death, the great leveller, comes to us all. There is some question as to whether the sentiments attributed to Lovekyn are actually his. Since it is likely that the brass was commissioned by his successor, Walworth, some years after his death, it may be that the words are actually Walworth's, and not those of Lovekyn himself. The similarity, however, between the sentiments on the brass and the austere provisions of the ordinances points to Lovekyn's ideas working through into the text. In each case, Lovekyn is shown to be concerned with his personal acceptability before God – in the case of the epitaph, his own acceptability, achieved through personal humility, and in the case of the ordinances, that of his chaplains, achieved through moral purity. If the inscription was actually commissioned by Walworth, it probably reflects Lovekyn's own thinking. Quite possibly, it reproduces part of the wording of the epitaph on Lovekyn's original alabaster tomb.

The wording of Lovekyn's epitaph, while distinctive, is not the product of a sensibility in any way singular or exceptional at this time. Personal self-abasement, contempt for the flesh and an emphasis on funerary austerity are the characteristics of a strain of piety which gained wide favour in the late fourteenth century. A similar contempt for the flesh is found in the wills of some upper-class testators of the period. In 1394 the Yorkshire knight Sir Brian Stapleton referred to his 'caitiff body', while five years later a Chancery clerk, Robert Folkingham, spoke of his 'wretched sinful body' to be 'buryen here in earth'. This ascetic piety was associated with a trend towards simpler funerals than before. In 1407, for example, the Wiltshire knight Sir William Stourton insisted on a simple burial for his 'putrid body, naked as it came into the world except for a linen cloth'.[5] The origins of this preoccupation with personal unworthiness are probably to be found in the penitential literature popular at the time. In the most widely disseminated such text, the *Prick of Conscience* of c.1360, the reader was urged to reflect on the wretchedness of man's condition and to prepare for death by contemplating the four last things: Death: Judgement, Heaven and Hell. A powerful stimulus to reflection was afforded by the penitential exercises sometimes prescribed by confessors to their patrons. The language of contempt for the body – specifically, the phrase 'food for worms' – is found in the penitential tract, *Le Livre de Seyntz Medicines*, written in 1354 by the king's cousin, Henry, duke of Lancaster.[6] There are other tomb epitaphs, in addition to Lovekyn's, on which the theme of the mortality of the flesh is picked up. In a borrowing from the Office of the Dead, the text 'de terre fu fait et en terre et a terre suy retourne' was used on brasses at Norbury (Staffordshire), Mereworth (Kent), Etchingham (Sussex) and Birdbrook (Suffolk).

It is to this background that we can make sense of the wording in the second phrase of Lovekyn's epitaph. The phrase 'fine food for worms' has its roots in the same ascetic mood as the contempt for the flesh found on the tomb epitaphs and in the wills of the more self-conscious testators of the day. Most of those who are found speaking in these terms were knights. What is remarkable in the case of the Lovekyn epitaph is that it is a townsman who is found uttering these sentiments. We know far less about the commemorative tastes of the townsmen than of the gentry because so many of their memorials have gone. The loss is greatest of all in London, where most of the pre-Reformation churches were destroyed in the Great Fire. The significance of the Lovekyn inscription to the historian is that it helps to fill a gap. It tells us something about the tastes of the urban elite in a period when religious sensibilities were subject to significant new influences. What it suggests is that in some cases at least those tastes may not have so very different from those of the gentry whose memorials we know so much more about.

## *Acknowledgements*

*I am grateful to Martin Stuchfield for help with the illustrations.*

**Notes**

1 J. Stow, *A Survey of London*, ed. C. L. Kingsford (2 vols., Oxford, 1908, repr. 2000), I, 219–20.

2 A. Heales, 'The History of the Free Chapel of St Mary Magdalene, Kingston-upon-Thames', *Surrey Archaeological Collections*, 8 (1883), 255–356.

3 Heales, 'History of the Free Chapel of St Mary Magdalene', 264–71.

4 *The Itinerary of John Leland*, ed. L. Toulmin-Smith (5 vols., London, 1909–10), IV, 86.

5 For these examples, see M. G. A. Vale, *Piety, Charity and Literacy among the Yorkshire Gentry, 1370–1480* (York: Borthwick Papers, 50, 1976), 11; K. B. McFarlane, *Lancastrian Kings and Lollard Knights* (Oxford, 1972), 213, 215.

6 *Le Livre de Seyntz Medicines*, ed. E. J. Arnould (Anglo-Norman Text Society, 1940), 4, 124.

# Commemoration in brass and glass of the Blackburn family of York

*Sally Badham*

*Sally Badham is President of the Church Monuments Society and the author of many publications on medieval church monuments.*

CHOICES FOR MONUMENTAL COMMEMORATION were subject, amongst other factors, to influence from the commemorative preferences of other family members. A preference for monumental brasses on the part of the Blackburn family of merchants of York (for a pedigree, see Fig. 1), can be traced largely through the evidence of their wills. They and their kin were also responsible for commissioning several windows in York churches, demonstrating another shared taste in commemoration.

The only surviving Blackburn monument is an indent of a lost brass to a civilian and two wives in the nave of St Mary Castlegate, York (Fig. 2). It is currently covered by an 'art installation' and thus inaccessible, the church now being used as an Arts Centre. The outlines of the indent enable it to be identified as the product of a local brass engraving workshop 'Yorkshire Series 1c' which was operational *c*.1405–30.[1] A worn low relief marginal inscription with corner quatrefoils completes the composition. Antiquarian notes enable this monument to be attributed to John Blackburn (d.1426) and his two wives,

*Fig. 1: Pedigree of the Blackburn family of York.*

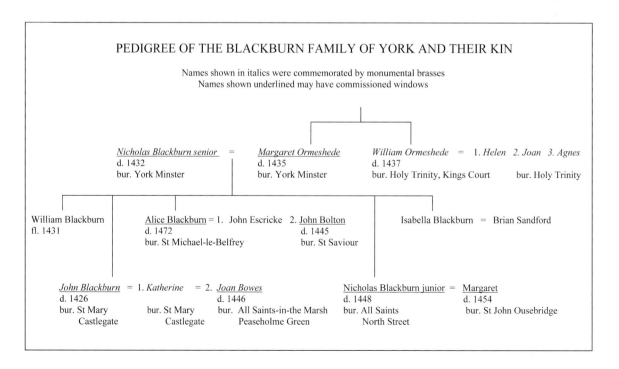

### PEDIGREE OF THE BLACKBURN FAMILY OF YORK AND THEIR KIN

Names shown in italics were commemorated by monumental brasses
Names shown underlined may have commissioned windows

Nicholas Blackburn senior = Margaret Ormeshede — William Ormeshede = 1. Helen 2. Joan 3. Agnes
d. 1432 — d. 1435 — d. 1437
bur. York Minster — bur. York Minster — bur. Holy Trinity, Kings Court — bur. Holy Trinity

William Blackburn fl. 1431 — Alice Blackburn = 1. John Escricke 2. John Bolton — Isabella Blackburn = Brian Sandford
d. 1472 — d. 1445
bur. St Michael-le-Belfrey — bur. St Saviour

John Blackburn = 1. Katherine = 2. Joan Bowes — Nicholas Blackburn junior = Margaret
d. 1426 — d. 1446 — d. 1448 — d. 1454
bur. St Mary Castlegate — bur. St Mary Castlegate — bur. All Saints-in-the-Marsh Peaseholme Green — bur. All Saints North Street — bur. St John Ousebridge

*Fig. 2: St Mary Castlegate, York, indent of lost brass to John Blackburn (d.1426) and his two wives, Katherine and Joan. Drawing (excluding worn incised inscription): Sally Badham*

Katherine and Joan. On 14 March 1669 Henry Johnston recorded:

> Circumscribed about a stone of marble in the middle isle of the church only this ... Johes Blakburne civis et mercator Ebor et Katherine uxor ejus quoru aiabs propt deus. There hath been 3 figures on it and an inscription on brass but torn of.[2]

Most of the extant effigial brasses from this workshop depict knights, but the worn brass at Wath to Richard Norton, Chief Justice of the King's Bench (d.1420) and his wife Katherine gives a reasonable indication of what the Blackburn brass would have been like (Fig. 3).

## Nicholas Blackburn senior

John was the eldest son of Nicholas de Blackburn who, when registered as a freeman in 1403 was described as being from Richmond, Yorkshire, although it is likely that his family originated in Blackburn, Lancashire. This elder Blackburn was a

merchant of the Staple of Calais and is recorded as exporting wool, hides and fleeces in very large quantities from Newcastle-upon-Tyne as well as cloth and coal; he also imported iron.[3] He amassed a considerable fortune from the profits of trade; the monetary bequests alone in his will amounted to £644. He owned property in both Richmond and York and held an important position in the York civic elite, becoming mayor in 1402. He was active in local affairs and was briefly, 'on the nomination of merchants of the realm', admiral of the Northern Fleet in 1406–7. He married Margaret Ormeshede (d.1435) by whom he had three sons and two daughters.

Nicholas made ample provision for the swift passage of his soul through Purgatory, in addition to the £310 devoted in his will to the health of his soul. In 1412 he founded a chantry in Richmond parish church and in 1414 he and his wife, Margaret, were admitted to the Corpus Christi guild at York. In 1432 the Dominican prior at York granted him a perpetual chantry at the altar of St Mary Magdalen in the priory church, a second chantry at the high altar and an obit to be celebrated on St James's day with a requiem on St Anne's day. In his will, Nicholas also mentions four other chantries in York: at the chapel of St William on Ouse Bridge, St John the Evangelist's church, and two in St Martin Micklegate. Nicholas died in 1432, after his eldest son John, but he was survived by his son Nicholas and daughter Alice.

Regarding his burial and commemoration, Nicholas directed in his will:

> Lego corpus meum sepeliendum in ecclesia Cathedrali beati Petri Ebor in australi parte coram ymagine dominae nostre ibidem sub lapide meo marmorio ad hoc in eodem loco preparato
> (I leave my body to be buried in the cathedral church of St Peter in York in the south part, before the image of Our Lady there, under my marble stone prepared for that purpose in the same place)

The wording 'marble stone' is fairly commonly found in wills and normally refers to a monumental brass. Nicholas's wife, Margaret (d.1435), also asked for burial with her husband 'sub lapide marmorio coram ymagine domine nostre ex parte australi inibi conquiestcentis' (beneath a marble stone before the image of Our Lady on the south side). No record can be traced of Nicholas and Margaret's brass, but the empty indent may be amongst those recorded by Torre, but destroyed in the eighteenth-century re-paving of York Minster.[4]

In the 1420s Nicholas Blackburn and his third son and namesake, Nicholas the younger, took a major part in commissioning a new window for All Saints, North Street, York.[5] Now in the east window, the glass was originally in the second window from the east of the north wall in the Choir of Our Blessed Virgin Mary (where the Corporal Acts of Mercy window is now).[6] Nicholas the elder and his wife are shown in the bottom right-hand donor panel, while Nicholas the younger and his wife occupy the bottom left-hand panel (Figs. 4 & 5). The window has not survived intact from the medieval period; the donor figures, apart from that of Blackburn senior, were largely replaced by Wailes in 1844, but it is believed that he copied the figures and inscriptions as accurately as possible, using the evidence of the seventeenth-century antiquaries who made detailed notes in the York city churches. Certainly these notes reflect what can now be seen. Dodsworth's notes of 1618–19 read:

> In the North window of the Quyer: A man kneeling on his brest gu. a lyon rampt chequi er. and erms. crowned or vnderneath this inscription: Orate pro aimabus Nicholai Blakborne senioris quondam Maior istius civitatis Ebor. et Margerete vxoris sue et omnium fidelium defunctorum. In the same window a man kneeling by him the coate aforsaid differenced wth a mollett or and under itt this inscription: Orate p aiabus Nicholai Blackborne Junioris et Margarete vxoris sue itaque pro animabus omnium benefectorum istius fenestre … luminare vitro.[7]

*Figs. 4 & 5: All Saints, North Street, York, donor figures in the east window. Fig. 4 (top): Nicholas Blackburn the younger and his wife. Fig. 5 (bottom): Nicholas Blackburn the elder and his wife. Photos: Sally Badham*

Torre confirmed in 1691:

> In ye N quire side window are the pictures of Nic. Blackburn & his
> lady kneeling at prayer. Nicholas Blackburn Sen. L.M. 1447. He in
> Armour with spurs on his heels w[th] a shield of his Arms upon his
> breast. And another over his head ut supra. An an Escrowle issuing out
> of his mouth containing *Det munus nobis Rex*. She w[th] her back to him
> holding a prayer-book in her hand wherin is written *dnes salva me a
> peccatis & Aperies et os meum*. Under both of them is inscribed *Orate pro
> aiabz Nicholai Blakborne senr quondam maioris Civitatis Ebor et Margerete
> uxis ejus*.
> In the next Light of the same Window are drawn the portraitures of
> Nicholas Blackburn jun. & his wife kneeling together. She holding a
> book open in her hands wherein is writ *dne in futore tuo judica me netz
> in ira tua*. And his shield of Arms by him is this viz. *Gu a lyon rampt
> checky Erm. & Sab. u[th] a mullett* on his breast.[8]

Matthew Hutton gave an abbreviated but consistent account in
1659 and the donor figures and inscriptions were also drawn by
Henry Johnston.[9]

The Blackburn arms are shown above the figures. To the left
of each donor pair is a shield with a letter 'B', evidently their
merchant's mark. The surviving sections of the inscription request
prayers for the souls of both generations of the Blackburn family.
That Blackburn senior was described as formerly mayor of York,
but that Nicholas junior's mayoralty in 1429 is not mentioned,
further helps to narrow the dating to between 1412 and 1427. The
inscription originally continued 'itaque pro animabus omnium
benefactorum istius fenestre luminare vitrio' (and so for the souls
of all the benefactors of this window light in glass)'.[10] Hence there
were other donors, but that only the Blackburns were depicted in
the window indicates that they bore the majority of the cost.

The religious content of the window was almost certainly
determined by Nicholas Blackburn senior. The central light
features St Anne teaching the Virgin to read, iconography echoed
by the donor panels in which the women are shown holding open
books. The figure of St Anne is flanked by Saints John the Baptist
and Christopher. Nicholas had a special devotion to all four saints.
In 1425 he gave prior John Wessington of Durham £10 of gold
to provide a memorial jewel in the image of St Anne,
St Christopher or St John the Baptist for the shrine of
St Cuthbert. In his will he commends his soul 'to almighty God
and to the blessed virgin Mary and her most holy mother Anne'.
His testamentary provisions included two wax torches to the
Guild of St Christopher in York. As mentioned above, his requiem
in York Minster was celebrated on St Anne's day and he was
buried in the Minster before an image of St Mary. He also refers
in his will to his chantry 'founded in the chapel of the most Holy

*Fig. 6: St Mary's, Beverley, Yorkshire, indent, probably to Henry and Nicholas Holme, both of whom died in 1471. Rubbing: Sally Badham*

Anne upon Foss Bridge in York'; this chapel was destroyed before any of the York antiquaries made notes, hence we have no knowledge of any artefacts he might have commissioned for it.

Nicholas Blackburn junior is shown in civil attire but wearing a dagger, while his father is in armour. The depiction of Nicholas senior in armour has generally been explained by his brief appointment as Admiral of the Northern Fleet, but representation in armour generally had more to do with perceived status than military activity.[11] The decision to have the head of the family shown in this way perhaps indicates their self-image as a family which was rising from modest roots to a position of wealth and gentry status within York society. They were, after all, armigerous. At the time that the window was commissioned, John Blackburn, Nicholas's eldest son was probably still alive. Nicholas junior was thus a younger son of lesser status, who would not have been appropriately shown other than in civil attire.

Although there is no remaining evidence of other merchants being similarly depicted in York, a parallel may be drawn with an indent in St Mary's, Beverley, Yorkshire, of a lost London F brass with two men in armour, probably Henry and Nicholas Holme, both of whom died in 1471 (Fig. 6). They were members of a

*Fig. 7  All Saints, North Street, York, Corporal Acts of Mercy window. Photo: Sally Badham*

long-standing family of Beverley merchants who had reached gentry status and had associations with knightly families. Henry was within the circle of the earl of Northumberland and at his death in 1471 two of the earl's retainers, Robert Constable of Flamborough and Ralph Hotham, were among his executors; the earl himself was supervisor of the will, in which Holme asks his executors to provide a 'marble stone', that is a brass, to cover his grave and that of his brother Nicholas.[12]

The glazing now in the east window of All Saints, York, is not the only window in the church donated by the Blackburns. There is antiquarian evidence that the Corporal Acts of Mercy window, now the second window from the east in the north aisle, but originally in the westernmost window of the north aisle, was a family donation (Fig. 7). Which generation is commissioned it uncertain, although Gee inclines to the elder Nicholas.[13] Certainly the Acts of Mercy are mentioned in Nicholas Blackburn senior's will. The panels have been rearranged to suit a three light rather than a two light window and some panels, including the canopies, have been taken from elsewhere. The bottom two panels originally contained the kneeling figure of Blackburn and his achievement of arms, as recorded by various antiquaries. The earliest, Dodsworth, saw:

In a window on the North of ye church: *G. a lyon raptchequi er. and ers. crowned or*, on a helme Ar. *a chappeau g. doubled Ar. on yeon a lyon passt. er. & ers. crowned or. mantled gu, doubled ar.* vnderneath this inscription *Orate pro anima Nicholai Blakborne cuius anime propicietur deus.*[14]

Torre also noted the kneeling donor figure of Blackburn.[15] Sadly these panels no longer survive, the donor figures now placed in this window being from other windows. On the left is Reginald Bawtree, who in 1429 left 100 shillings in his will for glazing; his figure was originally associated with the central window of the north aisle, known as St Thomas's window. On the right is a civilian couple from a window on the south side. The Corporal Acts of Mercy window may have lost its donor figures, but it is thought that the bearded man who carries out each Act of Mercy represents Nicholas Blackburn senior himself.

### Nicholas Blackburn junior

Nicholas Blackburn the younger (d.1448) became a freeman of York in 1402–3. He too worked his way up the York civic elite; he was a chamberlain in 1424, sheriff in 1427 and became mayor in 1429. In his will he touchingly asked to be buried:

*In choro beate Marie ubi sedere consuevi infra ecclesiam meam parochialem Omnoum Sanscotum in Northestrete in Ebor prope sepulcrum puerorum meorum*
(In the choir of St Mary where I was accustomed to sit within my parish church of All Saints in North Street in York near the tomb of my children buried there)

Nothing is known of the form that this lost monument took, although a floor monument is indicated, strongly suggesting a brass. It is significant that the glazing donated by the Blackburns and others, which is now in the east window, would originally have been placed near or over the place he was accustomed to sit in church and where he, his wife and his children were subsequently buried. Although this did not compare with the élite space of a chantry chapel partitioned off from the rest of the church by parclose screens, it did provide an association of this part of the church with the Blackburn family.

### Alice Bolton

Some years before 1430, Nicholas Blackburn senior's daughter, Alice, married John Bolton, a member of a family of Bolton mercers who had moved to York. He was another wealthy member of the York mercantile elite, becoming free of York in 1410 and enrolled in the Corpus Christi Guild in 1430. He was a chamberlain in 1417, sheriff in 1420 and mayor in 1410 and 1431. He also represented York in parliament in 1427 and 1428. As a merchant of the Staple of Calais, he dealt mainly in wool, although he also traded in cloth and other commodities. John died in 1445, followed by Alice in 1472.[16] Alice did not leave a will and John's is short and relatively uninformative. Although he names St John the Evangelist, Micklegate, as his parish church, he asked to be buried in St Saviour's following family tradition; in 1429, his brother William had also requested burial in St Saviour's, specifically in the tomb of his father, John Bolton. Unfortunately, no monument to any of the Boltons survives, nor is there any antiquarian evidence of any, although various unidentifiable indents were drawn by Torre. John and Alice Bolton also retained an interest in All Saints, North Street: a city inventory of 1509 records a chantry to John Bolton in this church, although the precise location is not given.

Barnett has suggested that the Boltons were patrons of the Prick of Conscience window at the east end of the north aisle of All Saints' church, although the evidence for this is circumstantial.[17] Her case rests on the bequest to Alice by her godfather, the chaplain William Revetour (d.1446), of a copy of the *Prick of Conscience*, which Barnett suggests could have been used as a basis for the iconography of the window. It is an attractive hypothesis, particularly given the Blackburn tradition of patronage of glazing in this church and elsewhere, but confirmatory documentary evidence is lacking and there are problems with the chronology. There are three sets of donors shown at the bottom of the window, but the once apparently extensive inscriptions below are now lost. That on the right shows a woman and two men; in 1670 an inscription remained under it commemorating Abel and Agnes Hessle, their daughter Cecily and her husband Roger Henryson.[18] The middle panel had a woman and two men, with in 1670 the inscription 'et dni H Hessyl' undoubtedly referring to Henry Hessel, Abel's father. Finally the left hand panel shows a man and two women; little of the inscription remained in 1670, but in 1659 Hutton recorded the name 'Wiloby'. He also recorded the arms of Saville elsewhere in the window. It is not impossible that the Boltons could have been the third set of patrons shown in the window, although the balance of probabilities is against it. The unknown donors are a man and his two wives, but John Bolton married only once.

Moreover, there is no record of any Willoughby or Saville in the family's pedigree. The glass could have been made after the couple's marriage, but no authority on medieval glass dates the window as late as the late 1440s, when widowed Alice Bolton was bequeathed the copy of the *Prick of Conscience*. Nor were other donors likely to have still been alive then. Abel Hessle was living in the parish in 1427 and is recorded up to 1437.[19]

## William Ormeshede

William Ormeshede (d.1437), the brother of Margaret Blackburn and one of Nicholas Blackburn senior's executors, was another merchant who moved up the civic hierarchy in York, becoming chamberlain in 1411, sheriff in 1415 and mayor in 1425 and 1433. He represented York in parliament in 1421, 1425 and 1430 and, like his sister and brother-in-law, was a member of the prestigious Corpus Christi Guild. In his will, he requested:

> *Corpusque meum sepeliendum infra ecclesiam parochialem sancte Trinitas in Curia Regis in Ebor' coram alteri sancte Marie virginis in eadem ecclesia iuxta corpus Johanne uxoris mee defuncte*
> (My body to be buried within the parish church of Holy Trinity in King's Court in York before the altar of St Mary the Virgin in the same church beside the body of Joan my deceased wife)

There is no mention of any monument in the will, but again there is evidence that they were commemorated by a lost brass. The church of Holy Trinity, King's Court, York, also sometimes known as Christchurch, was demolished in 1937; although some floor monuments, including indents of inscription brasses remain.[20] Dodsworth recorded a now lost inscription, almost certainly from a brass, which read:

> *Orate pro aiabz Willmi Ormeshede quondam maioris istius civitatis Eborum qui obiit xvj die mensis Septemnbris A dni MCCCCCXXXVIJ et p aiabus Elene Johanne et Agnetis uxoribus eius pro quibus omnibus dicatur Pater Noster cum Ave Maria ut eis propietur deus in secula infinita Amen.*
> (Pray for the soul of William Oremeshede formerly mayor of this city of York who died on the twenty-sixth day of the month of September AD 1437 and for the souls of Helen, Joan and Agnes, his wives for all of whom let there be said Our Father and Hail Mary that God may be merciful to them for endless ages.)[21]

## John Blackburn

Nicolas Blackburn the elder's eldest son, John Blackburn, became a freeman of York in 1402–3. When he was admitted to the Corpus Christi guild in 1412 he was described as a merchant alderman of the parish of St Mary Castlegate. Between 1417 and 1420 he was one of the twelve city aldermen. He also represented

York in parliament in 1417. He and his second wife, Joan, copied the example of his father and brother by commissioning a window recorded as being in St Cuthbert's church, Peaseholme Green, York. It possibly was originally in All Saints in the Marsh, Peaseholme Green, where his wife chose burial; in 1586 the benefices of the two churches were united and All Saints was demolished.[22] The window no longer survives;[23] but it was recorded by Roger Dodsworth:

> In the North window: A man kneeling in armor on his brest *G. a lyon ramp checqui er & ers crowned or a* [label of 3 points] about his necke his wief 3 sons & on ad and under all: *Orate pro animabus Johannis Blakborne et Johanne vxoris qui fecerimus istam fenestram.*[24]

In his will, John Blackburn requested:

> *Corpus meum ad sepeliendum in ecclesia parochiali beate Marie virginis in Castelgate in Ebor' iuxta corpus Katerine nuper uxoris mee et puerorum meorum*
> (my body to be buried in the parish church of St Mary Castlegate in York beside the bodies of Katherine my former wife and my children)

Since the indent (Fig. 2) and the antiquarian notes show that both wives were depicted on John Blackburn's brass, it is likely that he had already commissioned his monument, probably on Katherine's death. Although Joan Blackburn was shown on her husband's brass, she chose to be buried at All Saints, Peaseholme, although no separate monument to her survives or is known from antiquarian notes.

Although the window showed three sons and a daughter, they were not depicted on the brass. Probably the children did not survive John since none are mentioned in his will, but that would not normally preclude their representation. In contrast to London-made brasses, however, the products of the York brass engraving workshops did not feature figures of offspring shown as groups of diminutive figures shown below the main effigies. It is curious, moreover, that Blackburn chose to be shown on his brass in civilian dress but was depicted in the window in armour, implying an uncertainty as to his status in society. Perhaps when commissioning his brass he was conforming to practice in the circles in which he moved; antiquarian notes show that the York civic elite in the fifteenth century invariably appeared in civil dress on their monuments.

John Blackburn and his widow Joan, the daughter of the wealthy York merchant William Bowes, were evidently pious and wealthy - amongst the bequest in Joan's will were an alabaster devotional image and a primer - yet their expenditure on their funeral monument was comparatively modest. Although we cannot know how much John spent on this brass, comparisons with documented examples of the cost of contemporary brasses suggest that the brass in St Mary Castlegate probably cost around £10. The following wills give prices in the region of £10–14 for double brasses, some canopied:

> 1394 Sir Richard at Leese (Sheldwich, Kent) £10
> 1397 Sir John de St Quintin (Brandesburton,
>      Yorkshire) £13 6s 8d
> 1398 Sir Thomas Ughtred (Catton, Yorkshire) £10
> 1399 Sir Philip Darcy (Guisborough Priory, Yorkshire) £10
> 1420 Sir Arnald Savage (Bobbing, Kent) £13 6s 8d.[25]

Some variation is evident. In 1405 Thomas Graa of York evidently thought £5 adequate for a marble stone with brass images of himself and his wife, yet the executors' accounts for the estate of Thomas de Dalby, Archdeacon of Richmond, record a payment of £14 13s 4d for a simple brass with inscriptions and shields to be laid down in York Minster.[26]

A shield with the Blackburn's merchant's mark in the south chapel east window of St Mary Castlegate implies that John and Joan may have followed the example of other family members in commissioning a window in their parish church. Unfortunately the shield is not in its original position as all the surviving glass in the church, mostly fourteenth-century in date, has been re-set in this window. None of the antiquarian notes for St Mary's mention the shield, so they cannot help to provide a context for it.

## Conclusion

The burial practices and patronage of the prominent Blackburn family serves to illustrate that brasses, including products of the York workshops, were commissioned by the city's élite as well as those influential in the county. That members of the Blackburn family chose to be commemorated by brasses is not exceptional in itself for members of their class. Barnett has shown that in York, although those commemorated by surviving and recorded monuments, many of which were brasses, came from twenty different social categories, 44% of all recorded monuments in the city commemorated merchants.[27] Yet that John Blackburn chose a comparatively modest locally-made brass, rather than a metropolitan product, is more worthy of note.

The glazing commissioned by the members of the Blackburn family was provided in part to enrich their parish churches, but also to commemorate themselves and thus elicit prayers from the Christian faithful. Figures of the donors kneeling in prayer were inserted in the lower, more visible panels of the windows, accompanied by inscriptions asking for prayers for those shown. Yet the monuments and windows were only a small – and relatively inexpensive – part of the commemorative strategy of members of the Blackburn family. Throughout this paper mention has been made of some of the other arrangements they made to maximise the prayers that would be said for them to speed the progress of their souls though Purgatory. In part this was through good works and charitable gift-giving, in return for which they would have expected prayers. Yet these provisions, like the provision of church fittings, such as glazing schemes and the provision of tomb monuments, although likely to elicit prayers, could not guarantee them. Hence, like many of their contemporaries, the Blackburns and their kin channeled far more of their available funds into organised intercession, largely through the setting up of chantries, involvement in religious guilds and the funding of soul masses.

The Blackburn family and their kin undoubtedly thought that the Catholic faith and the associated guilds, religious houses and soul masses would last for ever. Yet within a century there had been a religious revolution. In consequence, the fruits of all their expenditure on charitable gift-giving, chantries and soul masses are long gone, in some cases along with the associated churches. All that now remains to memorialise this prominent York family is one indent in St Mary Castlegate and the east window of All Saints, North Street.

### Notes

1  S. Badham, 'Monumental brasses: the development of the York workshops in the fourteenth and fifteenth centuries', in C. Wilson (ed.) *Medieval Art, Architecture and Archaeology in the East Riding of Yorkshire* (British Archaeological Association Conference Proceedings, 1989), 165–85.

2  Henry Johnston 'Church notes and drawings' (1669–71), Bodleian Library, Oxford, MS Top Yorks C14, fol. 104. The indent was also recorded in the broadly contemporary notes by James Torre, 'Antiquities ecclesiastical of the city of York', York Minster Library, MS L1(8), fol. 386; and, using the church notes of earlier antiquaries, by F. Drake, *Eboricum or the History and Antiquities of the City of York* (1738, repr. Wakefield, 1978), 286.

3  For Nicholas Blackburn, see J. Kermode, *Medieval Merchants. York, Beverley and Hull in the Middle Ages* (Cambridge, 1998), 335; for the Blackburn family including transcripts of their wills see A. Rycraft et. al. (eds.), *The Blackburns in York. Testaments of a Merchant Family in the Later Middle Ages* (York, 2006).

4  James Torre, 'The antiquities of York Minster', York Minster Library, MS L1(7).

5  P. J. Shaw, *An old York Church. All Hallows in North Street* (York, 1908), 30–31. For more about the connection between the Blackburns and All Saints church see P. S. Barnwell, C. Cross and A. Rycraft, *Mass and Parish in late Medieval England: The Use of York* (Reading, 2005), *passim*.

6  E. A. Gee, 'The painted glass of All Saints' church, North Street, York', *Archaeologia* 102, 151–202.

7 Roger Dodsworth, , 'Yorkshire church notes' 1618–32, Bodleian Library, Oxford, MS Dodsworth 157, fol.17.

8 Torre, MS L(1)8, fol. 624–25.

9 Matthew Hutton, 'Antiquities of Yorkshire', York Minster Library, L 14, fol. 26 and Bodleian Library, Oxford, MS Top Yorks C14, fol. 94v.

10 MS Dodsworth 157, fol. 17.

11 R. Almond, 'All Saints' church, York, the Blackburn window: a medieval conundrum', *Medieval Life*, 1 (Winter, 1995), 26–30.

12 J. Raine, (ed.), *Testamenta Eboracensia part 3 1395–1491*, Surtees Society, 45 (York, 1865), 192–95.

13 Gee, 'All Saints', 187–89.

14 MS Dodsworth 157, fol.17.

15 Torre, MS L(1)8, fol. 624.

16 Although Alice did not leave a will, her date of death is recorded in a Book of Hours of the Use of York, now in York Minster, known as the Bolton Hours, along with the dates of death of her husband. The Boltons were not the original owners of the book. The first owners are depicted in the manuscript but their names are unknown.

17 C. M. Barnett, 'Commemoration in the parish church; identity and social class in late medieval York', *Yorkshire Archaeological Journal*, 72 (2000), 73–92 (pp. 84–85).

18 Gee, 'All Saints', 161–62, 187 and 198.

19 RCHME, *York: Vol. 3 South West of the Ouse* (1972), 8.

20 B. Wilson and F. Mee, *The Medieval Parish Churches of York. The Pictorial Evidence* (York, 1998), 44–47.

21 MS Dodsworth 157, fol.13v.

22 Wilson and Mee, *Medieval Churches of York*, 37.

23 F. Harrison, *The Painted Glass of York* (1927), 158–59.

24 MS Dodsworth 157, fol. 21.

25 R. H. d'Elboux, 'Testamentary brasses', *Antiquaries Journal* 29 (1959), 183–91, (pp.189–90); see also N. Saul, 'The contract for the brass of Richard Willoughby (d.1471) at Woolaton (Notts.)', *Nottingham Medieval Studies* 50 (2006), 166–193 (p. 178).

26 H. Haines, *Manual of Monumental Brasses* (1861, reprinted Bath, 1970), lviii; S. Badham, 'The lost brass to Thomas de Dalby, archdeacon of Richmond, 1400, in York Minster, Yorkshire', *Monumental Brass Society Bulletin*, 111 (May 2009), 213–14.

27 Barnett, 'Commemoration in the parish church', 76 and 78.

# 'Flouds are due unto this stone': English verse epitaphs at Alderton, Wiltshire

*Jon Bayliss*

*Jon Bayliss, recently retired from a career in Information Technology, has been interested in church monuments since 1971.*

BETWEEN 1717 AND 1719 John Le Neve published five volumes entitled *Monumenta Anglicana*.[1] The sub-titles described them as *Being inscriptions on the monuments of several eminent persons*, each volume devoted to recording the inscriptions of those who died during a particular range of years. The volumes cover the years 1600–1718 and provide an opportunity to compare types of commemorative inscriptions over a period of almost 120 years. The volume covering the earliest period, 1600–1649, has significantly more inscriptions containing verse in English than the other volumes, which is not entirely surprising as it was the age of William Shakespeare (1563–1616), John Donne (1572–1631) and Ben Jonson (1572–1637). While Shakespeare's contribution to the genre is less than clear cut,[2] published verse collections by Donne and Jonson included epitaphs, as did those by other contemporary poets.

Many epitaphs produced at this period were not necessarily intended to be engraved on monuments of those commemorated in the verses, but to hang on boards nearby. Donne's close friend, Christopher Brooke (*c.*1570–1628), produced a verse epitaph which was recorded as hanging in the church of St James, Clerkenwell, but his name also appears engraved in brass as the author of an epitaph to Dorothy Brewster at Willingale Doe, Essex.[3] While Brooke's verse was not well-regarded outside of Donne's circle, the very best verse epitaphs on tombs reflect the high standard of much contemporary poetry. However, almost all of it is anonymous. In instances where the same verses appear on different monuments, they are likely to be stock verses provided by the sculptor. One major tomb sculptor of the period, Edward Marshall, was a friend of the poet Francis Quarles but one would be most hesitant to attribute to him verses that Marshall used repeatedly.

An exception to this general pattern of anonymity is to be found in St Giles' church, Alderton, Wiltshire where at least four monuments have verses of known authorship. John Aubrey, the Wiltshire historian best known for his *Brief Lives*, is the source of the information, first published in 1821 by Sir Thomas Phillipps.[4] Aubrey was, for a considerable time, a friend of Thomas Gore of Alderton (1632–1684), a fellow antiquarian, although the two men later fell out. Many members of Gore's family are commemorated at Alderton. In 1659, a number of Wiltshire antiquaries agreed to cooperate on a history of their county, to be modeled on Dugdale's then recently published work on Warwickshire. William Yorke was to undertake the middle part of the county and Aubrey the north, with Thomas Gore and others acting as assistants. Aubrey evidently obtained his information on Alderton from Thomas, the eldest surviving son of Charles Gore and Lydia White.

The monuments with English verse epitaphs begin with that to Thomas's aunt, Ann, who married Gyles James and died at the age of forty in 1629 after three years of marriage. Her black marble ledger stone (Fig. 1) is a type of monument that was gaining popularity in the 1620s and is undoubtedly London work. As with some other early black ledger stones, the factual part of the inscription is cut around the margins of the slab, with verses and biblical quotations set in the centre.

Expectans expectavi Psal: 40.

With Jacob's Rahel, I (a James his wife)
Waited full long before our married life.
In mee it was a match-lesse expectation
More tædious farre, till matches consumation;
W<sup>ch</sup> once enjoy'd, and scarce three yeares in all,

*Fig. 1: Ledger stone to Ann James (d.1629), Alderton, Wiltshire.*

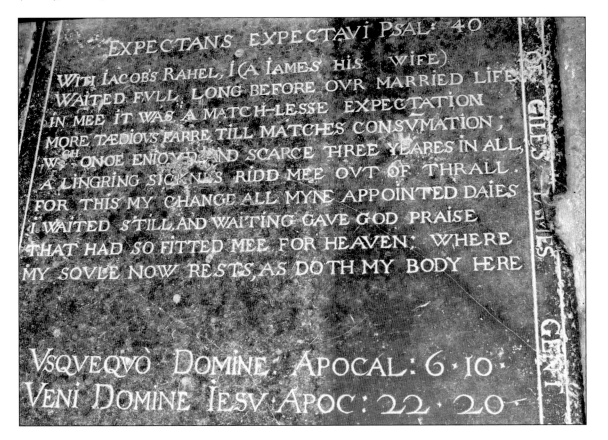

*Fig. 2: Mural monument with brasses to Ann (d.1636) and William James (d.1637), Alderton, Wiltshire.*

A lingring sicknes ridd me out of thrall.
For this my change all myne appointed daies
I waited still, and waiting gave God praise
That had so fitted mee for Heaven; where
My soule now rests, as doth my body here

Usque quo Domine: Apocal: 6. 10.
Veni Domine Jesu. Apoc: 22: 20.

One of her sexes worthies here doth lie,
A wife, a patterne to posterity:
To husband loyall, courteous unto all,
Pious to God, to th' poore most liberall.

Aubrey gives no author for these verses, which predate Thomas Gore's birth in March 1631/2 and were clearly written specifically for Ann James. The second example is more general but does not appear to be a stock verse although the sentiments are entirely typical of the period. These verses commemorate another Ann James, in this case Thomas Gore's grandmother.

> Dear Saint of God to whom in life most Deare
> Gods howse and messingers, and servants were
> The Holy things of God most precious all,
> Precious with God her death and buriall.
> Her Soule inlarg'd and Set at liberty
> The Seventi[e]th yeare of its Captivity,
> If evidence for Heaven be truth of grace
> Then Sure in heaven this Matron hath a place;
> Let after ages say when this is gonne
> Blest be the memorie of Such a one.

Two words of the verse differ in the published transcription, but those two words change that line into nonsense. Either Aubrey or Phillips incorrectly transcribed the sixth line as 'The *seaventeenth* yeare of *her* captivitie'.

Ann's brass is set in a well cut freestone wall monument (Fig. 2) alongside that of her husband, William James. She died on 20 December 1636, aged 70, he on 28 March 1637, aged 56, little more than three months later. However, his brass is of provincial quality, unlike hers, which, despite occasional imperfections in the way the verses are set out is clearly metropolitan in origin. His inscription (Fig. 3) begins, like his wife's, 'An epitaph on the death of'.

> Death parteth soule and body man and wife,
> So as to meet againe in better life,
> On better termes; meane while o[u]r bodies must
> To their first nothing turne at best but dust,
> Till glorified, our soules doe alwaies sing
> All glory to the everlasting King.

*Fig. 3: Brass to William James (d. 1637), Alderton, Wiltshire.*

This verse is separated by an engraved foliage band from the next.

> Surviveing friends in life see you prepare
> For life in Heav'n where no survivors are,
> That when of this short life death ends ye story
> You sharers be with us of endlesse glory.

William's verses are the first for which Aubrey gives an author, Parson Noble, of Sutton Benger, but given the short period between two deaths and the shared monument, Noble presumably wrote those for William's wife Ann too, and probably the 1629 verses to the earlier Ann James also. William Noble was born in Yorkshire around 1595 and educated at Oxford at Magdalen Hall, and Queen's College. He was subsequently the incumbent of a number of parishes in the neighborhood of Alderton: vicar of Malmesbury St Paul in 1619, rector of both Luckington and Oldbury in 1621, and vicar of Sutton Benger in 1637. He resigned the latter. His successor was instituted on 25 March 1640.[5]

Thomas Gore's sister Elizabeth died, aged four, on 14 April 1641. Her brass (Fig. 4) is set into a freestone slab on the floor of the chancel, now partly covered and includes a verse epitaph 'by Mr Parson Noble of Sutton Benger'.

> So rare a piece for bewty, grace, and witt,
> Though God had shewed us yet he thought not fitt
> For us to gaze upon too long: twas hee
> That tooke her to himself, himself to see:
> Admired she was by all that did behold her,
> Much more shall be when God anew shall mould her.

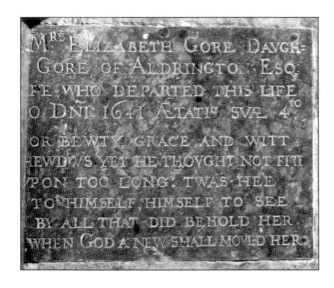

Fig. 4: Brass to Elizabeth Gore
(d. 1641), Alderton, Wiltshire.

Elizabeth was also commemorated by a brass set up in 1641 that was also to the memory of two of her brothers and two of her sisters. The verse on the brass is also by Noble and relates to the biblical text chosen to precede it.

> Malachy 3. 17 They shall be mine, saith the Lord of Hostes, in that day when I make up my Jewells.
>
> Jewells of price this place contains,
> As a choice Cabinet. The Remaines
> Of those sweet soules all of a Race,
> Which now in Heaven have their place.

This brass is set in a mural tablet evidently by the same mason that made the tablet for William and Ann James and was formerly

*Fig. 5: Mural monument to Charles Gore (d.1628), Alderton, Wiltshire.*

set near the sculpted monument with a kneeling figure (Fig. 5) to Charles Gore, the eldest son, who died in 1628, who is also commemorated by the brass. Their father Charles, who died on 11 November 1649 aged 56, has, surprisingly, only a small freestone slab with a simple unascribed verse.[6]

> By sinn came death
> Death brought me to the grave
> By Christ came life
> My sinfull soule to save

The sequence ends with the much more impressive London-made floor brass (Fig. 6) of Lydia Gore, who died on 3 January 1654/5. Aubrey names Dr Tully as the author of her verses.

*Fig. 6: Ledger stone to Lydia Gore (d. 1654/5), Alderton, Wiltshire.*

Reader if thou hast a teare
Doe not grudge to drop it here.
Thinke not it can fall alone,
Flouds are due unto this stone;
Here lies (ah how that word does pierce
And double blacks the mournfull herse)
Vertue's faire copy, Heaven's delight,
Not fitt for mens but angels sight.
In whose pure brest sweete innocence
(Exil'd by most) found sure defence.
Where no black thought, the sire of shame
(Charm'd by her vertues magick) came.
Lov'd by the Rich, the poore did blesse
Her, as their soveraigne almonesse.
Wife, Mother, Friend, better no age
E're showed upon the worlds stage.
Then Reader, if thou hast a teare
Canst thou chuse but drop it here.

Thomas Tully was born in Carlisle in 1620 and educated at Queen's College, Oxford, eventually becoming principal of St Edmund Hall in 1658. He was made a chaplain in ordinary to Charles II and in 1675 dean of Ripon but died a few months later. He was buried at Grittleton, a parish adjoining that of Alderton, where he had become rector in 1658. Earlier he had been master of Tetbury School, Gloucestershire, where his pupils included Thomas Gore.[7] Gore numbered Tully among his friends in later life. Tully's published theological works are extensive and he seems also to have had a reputation as a poet, composing a poem in French in 1643 to welcome the return of Henrietta Maria to England and a verse epitaph in Greek, hung over the grave on Lancelot Dawes, vicar of Barton in Westmoreland, who died in 1653/4. His epitaph for Lydia Gore seems to be the only poem in English to have come down to us, evidently written at Thomas Gore's request. Although he evidently took his initial inspiration from Thomas Randolph's opening lines of *Epitaph for Mistress IT*, he soon struck off in his own direction. Given the quality of his verse, it is a great pity that no more is identifiable.

Thomas Gore compiled a family register, in which he recorded in painstaking detail births, marriages and deaths and other events. Some of this detail no doubt came from older members of his family or from earlier documents. Of his younger sister Anna he recorded that William Noble, minister of God's Word at Oldbury near Didmarton, preached at her baptism in January 1638 and that she was married to John Scrope of Castle Combe by Thomas Tully in February 1662. Anna's eldest and fifth sons both had Thomas Tully and Thomas Gore as godfathers.[8] It is clear that William Noble and Thomas Tully were close to the Gore family through two generations and that the memorial verses they composed were, in part, personal tributes. William Noble's verse is representative of the mainstream of funeral epitaphs of the period but Thomas Tully's is a match for the best. Although Thomas Gore's own monument is a brass with a verse epitaph set in a mural monument, the verse is in Latin, bringing the tradition of English verse epitaphs at Alderton to an end.

## Notes

1  J. Le Neve, *Monumenta Anglicana*, 5 vols. (1717–19).
2  S. Watney, 'Sky aspiring pyramids', *Church Monuments*, 20 (2005), 103–10.
3  J. Strype, *Survey of London*, 2 vols. (1720), II.iv, 65. Lack, Stuchfield & Whittemore, *The Monumental Brasses of Essex* (2003), 912–13.
4  T. Phillipps, *Aubrey's collections for Wilts* (1821), 22–25. Verse transcriptions taken from this source have been corrected from photographs for the current article, except where the letter 'v' is 'u' in modern usage.
5  J. Foster, *Alumni Oxonienses: the members of the University of Oxford, 1500–1714*, 4 vols. (1891), III, 1073.
6  Although his monument is recorded in a facsimile edition of a book by Sir Thomas Phillipps, the verse is omitted (P. Sherlock (ed.), *Monumental Inscriptions of Wiltshire 1822*, Wiltshire Record Society, 53 (2000), 48). Sherlock notes that Phillips was often inaccurate.
7  Foster, *Alumni*, IV, 1515.
8  G. P. Scrope, *History of the manor and ancient barony of Castle Combe, in the county of Wilts* (1852), 311–13. Scrope observes that 'The monuments of the Gore family in Alderton Church are very numerous, and have been well preserved through the recent alteration of the fabric'.

# He loved his mother: memorials to mothers in the Early Modern period

*Jean Wilson*

*Jean Wilson, FSA formerly taught in the English Department of Boston University (USA) and has written extensively about Early Modern funerary monuments.*

IN 1581 THE ARCHBISHOP OF YORK, Edwin Sandys, was subjected to humiliating blackmail. He was staying in an inn in Doncaster, kept by two of his former servants, named Sysson, when Mrs Sysson climbed into bed with him, only to be 'surprised' by her husband and a young Yorkshire gentleman, Sir Robert Stapleton (married to Olive Talbot of Lacock Abbey, and so brother-in-law of Grace, Lady Mildmay, whose magnificent monument is to be seen at Apethorpe, Northamptonshire). The rights of the case are impossible to discern: Stapleton and his wife were nasty pieces of work who forced her father on his deathbed to disinherit the stunningly good Grace, but there had been gossip about Sandys and Mrs Sysson while she was in his service at Bishopthorpe. Stapleton and the Syssons demanded money; the archbishop unwisely paid up, the blackmailers (of course) demanded more and Sandys was eventually forced to go to the Privy Council, with the result that the blackmailers were punished and Sandys got his money back, but became notoriously ridiculous. Perhaps because of this Sandys was buried not in York Minster, but at Southwell, Nottinghamshire, where his tomb-chest provides a background for figures of his second wife, Cecily, whom he married in 1559, and their children (Fig. 1).[1]

The scandal may also provide an explanation for the fact that when that wife died in 1610 she was buried not with her husband but at Woodham Ferrers, Essex where she had passed her widowhood in the splendid new house Sandys had built at a property brought to him by his first wife, his cousin, Mary Sandys. Sandys's own temperament may provide another explanation for Cecily's burial apart from him – he managed to quarrel with almost every one of his friends during his career, and despite her being 'faier, well nurtured, sober and demure' and the evidence of conjugal affection afforded by nine children, he cannot have been easy to live with.

In 1619 Cecily's eldest son, Sir Samuel Sandys, erected an exquisite monument to her (attributed to William Wright of Charing Cross) at Woodham Ferrers (Figs. 2a & b). She kneels on a sarcophagus, in an arbour trailed with clematis:[2] above it Victories hold a wreath of laurel which encircles a lozenge with her arms. Pillars of touch with Corinthian capitals are surmounted

*Fig. 1: Monument to Archbishop Edwin Sandys (d.1588), Southwell Minster, Nottinghamshire (detail).*
*Photo: Norman Hammond*

by balls of the same flower-wreathed trelliswork. The monument is flanked by figures of Time and Death (the latter now missing).[3] The inscriptions celebrate her as a model Christian matron and, while naming her other children, emphasise her eldest son's devotion:

[*centre*]

CECILIE SANDYS, DAVGHTER
OF THOMAS WILLFORD OF CRAMBROOK IN
KENT ESQ:, SISTER TO Y[E] WORTHIE SOVLDIERS
S[R]: IAMES WILLFORD & S[R]: THOMAS WILLFORD WAS
WIFE TO EDWIN SANDYS ARCHBISHOP OF YORKE WHO
DIED IN GREAT HONOR IN Y[E] YEARE 1588 WHEN HE HAD
LYVED FVLL 70 YEARES. SHE LIVED A PVRE MAID 24 YEAR[S]
A CHAST & LOVING WIFE 29 YEAR[S]: A TRVE WIDOW 22 YEAR[S]:
TO HIR LAST. SHE BARE HIM 7 SONS & 2 DAVGH[RS]: SHE LED
A MOST CHRISTIAN & HOLY LIFE CAREFVLLY EDVCATED HIR
CHILD·: WISEL[Y]: GOVRNED HIR FAMILIE: CHARITABLY RELIEVED
THE POORE & WAS A TRVE MIRROR OF A CHRISTIAN MATRON
SHE DEP[R]TED THIS LIFE CONSTANT IN CHRISTIAN FAITH
5 FEB[R]: 1610 AT Y[E]: RISING OF Y[E]: SVN: HIR BLESSED SOVLE
ASCENDING TO Y[E]: CONSORT OF Y[E]: BLESSED AND HIR
BODIE LYETHE HEER INTERRE EXPECTING
THE IOYFVLL RESVRRECTION.

[*above left*]

[*SAM*]VELL SANDYS K[T]: ELDEST [*SON OF*]
Y[E]; SAID CICELY WHO OF HIS LOVE
[*AND*] PIETIE TO HIS SAID MOTHER HATH
AT HIS OWNE COST ERECTED
THIS MONVMENT IN Y[E]: YEARE
OF OVR LORD 1619 BEING
THEN HIGH SHERIFE OF
Y[E]: COVNTY OF WORCEST[R]:

[*above right*]

S:[R] EDWIN SANDYS K:[T] HER 2 SONNE
S:[R] MILES SANDYS K:[T] & BARÕ:[T] 3 SONNE
WILLIÃ: SAND[S] WHO DIED IN HIS YOVTH
THOMAS SANDYS ESQ: 5 SONNE
HENRY SANDYS ESQ: 6 SONNNE
GEORGE SANDYS ESQ: 7 SON
MARGARET MARRIED TO ANTHONY
ANCIER OF BOVRNE IN KENT ESQ:
ANN HIR 2 DAVGHT:[R] MARRIED TO
S:[R] WILLIÃ BARN OF WOLWICH

While the arbour provides a useful model for anyone interested in garden history, the most remarkable aspect of the monument is its visual symbolism. The septuagenarian Cecily Sandys, mother of nine, is presented with imagery associated with the Blessed Virgin Mary (BVM). The BVM is frequently depicted within an arbour and it is one of the common characterisations of her in medieval poetry and art. Moreover a common name for the native clematis Clematis vitalba was 'virgin's bower'.[4] It is well known that Marian imagery was transferred to Elizabeth I: here is an example of its being used in a non-royal context and with the emphasis not on Mary as Virgin, but on Mary as Mother. Even in the context of Protestantism the BVM provided a body of visual imagery which could be mined by those seeking to express the virtues of motherhood.

Monuments document emotional history. That Samuel Sandys chose to erect a monument to his mother shows that he cared for her: the imagery of the monument in which she is invested with the attributes of the Queen of Heaven shows the depth of his affection. Conventionally a widow would appear on her husband's tomb (as Cecily Sandys does), the responsibility for the erection of which, if it had not been erected in the subject's lifetime, or according to instructions in his will, lay with his heirs. Deviations from this pattern often indicate the nature of the relationship behind it. A widow might choose to pay for her husband's memorial herself in order to show her affection, as at Colmworth, Bedfordshire, where the monument to Sir William Dyer (d.1621) records that Lady Dyer 'in her life at her owne charge out of her loyal respect to her husband did erect this monument Ano. Dni. 1641'. A grandmother might choose to commemorate a loved grandchild, as at Cranborne, where the monument to the schoolboy John Elliot (d.1641) was erected by his grandmother, Lady Norton. Lady Savile erected (before 1627) a dynastic monument to herself and her descendants at St Nicholas Hurst, Berkshire, the home of her youngest daughter by her first marriage, on which she explains that 'She erected this monument whilst she was yet livinge for her selfe & hers beinge desirous to deposite her body in y$^e$ place where liveinge she had found soe much content & soe sweet a repose of her age'. The monument fitted well with the interests of her son-in-law, Sir Richard Harrison, who had erected a number of ancestral monuments in the church. Other women memorialised themselves for more selfish reasons. Mary Anne Childe (d.1659) wrote the smug epitaph which appears on her tomb at Blockley, Worcestershire in celebration of her virtues and her example to posterity.[5]

Fig. 2a: Monument (1619) attributed
to William Wright, to Cecily Sandys
(d. 1610), Woodham Ferrers, Essex.
From Frederic Chancellor, The
ancient sepulchral monuments of
Essex: a record of interesting tombs
in Essex churches and some
account of the persons and families
connected with them (London,
C.F. Kell, 1890), Plate cxliv.

Fig. 2b: Woodham Ferrers, Essex,
detail of the illustration of the
monument shown in Figure 2a.

There may have been a particularly close link between mothers and adult daughters, with mutual memorialisation. The inscription on the monument to Lady Russell of Thornhaugh (d.1611) now at Chenies, Buckinghamshire (originally at Watford) encapsulates the grief of all whose children predecease them:

> dame Dorothie Morrison her most lovinge & affectionate mother, s'vivinge contrarie to yᵉ ordinarie covrse of nature, & her owne harts desier hir most deere & most deerelie lovinge & beloved daughter hath for yᵉ laste office, & for an aeternall pledge of her motherlie love & affection in yᵉ hope of a gloriovs & ioyfull resurrection, consecrated ys monument.

The memorials of daughters to mothers, such as Lady Anne Clifford's beautiful monument to her mother, Margaret, Countess of Cumberland (d.1616, monument 1617) at Appleby, Westmoreland, are widely known, and, like Lady Savile, mothers often did end their lives living with a daughter and being buried at her home.

Sons and mothers are, however, not thought of as close. The son often left home and his mother's care at a young age, and the widowed mother's jointure might well be an annoying tax on the son's estate.[6] For a son individually to commemorate a previously unmemorialised mother might seem an implicit reproach to a surviving father whose duty it should have been, and where the son who does this is not the heir, there may also be an indication of dereliction on the part of the elder brother who had also failed in this duty. Funerary monuments as documents in emotional history may be evidence of bad feeling as well as of good. Something of this may be behind the monument to Gertrude, countess of Kingston (d.1649) at Holme Pierrepont, Nottinghamshire. The monument has no effigy, but is surmounted by a coffin with a gilt coronet (Fig. 3):

> *Here lyeth the illustrious Princess* GERTRUDE *Countesse of* KINGSTONE, *daughter to* HENRY TALBOT ESQˢ *son to* GEORGE *late Earle of* SHREWSBURY *she was married to the most Noble & Excellent* LOᴰ ROBERT *Earle of* KINGSTONE, *one of the Generalls to* KING CHARLES *the first in the late unhappy differences and in that service lost his life. she had by him many children. most dead there are living* HENRY MARQUIS *of* DORCHESTER, WILLIAM & GERVAS PIERREPONT ESQˢ & *one*

*daughter the Lady* ELIZABETH PIERREPONT. *she was a lady replete with all qualities that adorn her sex & more eminent in them than in the greatnes of her birth. she was most devoute in her dutyes to* GOD, *most observant of those to her neighbour an incomparable wife, a most indulgent mother & most charitable to those in want. in a word her life was one continued act of virtue she hath left a memory that will never dye & an example that may be imitated but not easily equall'd. She died in the* LXI *yeare of her age* A°. D. 1649 *and this monument was erected to her by her son* GERVAS PIERREPONT.

Gervas Pierrepont was the only one of the surviving children named on the monument to remain unmarried: he died in Holland in 1679, 'bequeathing £10,000 to the first member of his family who should obtain the honour and title of a duke'.[7] His patronage of his mother's monument may be an indication that he was particularly close to her but could also be a result of the fact that having no family he could better afford it than his siblings.

*Fig. 3: Monument to Gertrude Countess of Kingston (d. 1649), Holme Pierrepont, Nottinghamshire. Engraving by J. Wigley from Robert Thoroton,* The Antiquities of Nottinghamshire, *3 vols. (Nottingham, C. Burbage, 1790), vol. 1, facing p. 180.*

While the Countess of Kingston's monument certainly extols her as the model of women, mothers and wives, she is not, unlike Cecily Sandys, invested with imagery suggesting a superhuman virtue. Nor is her kinswoman Anne Keighley (d.1598), wife of William Cavendish (later first earl of Devonshire), who is buried at Ault Hucknall, Derbyshire with a sadly mutilated monument of very high quality, comprising a tomb chest surmounted by allegorical figures of Modesty, Prudence, Love/Charity, Obedience and Piety (Fig. 4).[8] The inscription reads:

1627

M.S.

IN HAC ARCA SUB SIGILIS

PUDICITIAE, PRUDENTIAE, AMORIS, OBSEQVENTIAE, PIETATIS

ANCILLANTIUM VIGILANTIUMQ VIRTUTUM

SITI, AC SERVATI SUNT CINERES

LECTISSIMAE DOMINA

ANNE KIGHLEIAE, HENRICI DE KIGHLEY, IN AGRO EBORACENSI

ARMIGERI, FILIAE ET HAEREDIS

QUAE PRAENOBILI GUILIELMO CAVENDISIO ARMIGᵒ: A CHATSWORTH

(IN COMITEM DEVONIAE POSTEA ERECTO)

NUPTA, GENUIT ILLI TRES FILIOS,

GILBERTÚ, GUILIELMÚ, ET JACOBÚ,

TOTIDEMQ FILIAS, MARIAM, ELIZABETHÃ

ET FRANCISCÃ FILIORUM JACOBUS NATU

MINIMUS IUXTA MATREM DORMIT.

GUILIELMUS COMES DEVONIAE, ET BARO

DE HARDWICK, HAERES ET SOLUS IAM

SUPERSTES MAT. CHARISS: (FRATREM [sic]

SORORUM VNA MEMORIAM CONSERVARE

VOLENS).

H.M.F.C.

OBIIT MENSE FEBRUARIO, ANNI

SALUTIS MDXCVIII.

(*Translation*: In this this casket under the images of Chastity, Prudence, Love, Obedience and Piety – the virtues which attended on and watched over her – are placed and preserved the remains of the most excellent lady Anne Keighley, daughter and heiress of Henry Keighley of Yorkshire, gentleman. Who, having been given in marriage to the most noble William Cavendish, gentleman, of Chatsworth (later raised to the Earldom of Devonshire), bore him three sons, Gilbert, William and James, and the same number of daughters, Mary, Elizabeth and Frances. James, the youngest of the sons, sleeps beside his mother.

William, Earl of Devonshire and Baron Hardwick, the heir and now the only survivor, wishing to preserve the memory of his dearest mother, together with that of his brothers and sisters, had this monument made. She died in February 1598.)

This assemblage presents the image of an ideal woman. The virtues resemble those attendant on Womanhood in Edmund Spenser's *The Faerie Queene*, (IV. x. 48–52), Shamefastness, Cheerfulness, Modesty, Courtesy, Silence and Obedience. The lack of any representation of Anne Keighley both defines her through her virtues and turns her into a generalised figure of the Good Woman: this is not just what Anne Keighley was, but what all women should aspire to be.

There may, however, be a subtext to this monument. After the death of Anne Keighley, William Cavendish remarried. His only son by this second marriage, Sir John Cavendish, died at the age of eleven in 1617 (he had been knighted as one of the companions of Henry, Prince of Wales) and has an impressive monument by John Colt at Chesham, Buckinghamshire. None of his elder half-siblings seem to have been so commemorated. When the first earl of Devonshire died in 1626 his successor not only erected the monument at Ault Hucknall to his mother, but also a double-monument at Edensor to his father and his uncle Henry Cavendish (d.1616): the latter comprises an iconographic exploration of the active and contemplative life, and the way in which service to the state may be either military (Henry Cavendish) or civil (William Cavendish). This monument combines with Ault Hucknall's presentation of female virtue in Anne Keighley to provide a moral programme which relates to other Early Modern programmes of virtue, such as Spenser's *The Faerie Queene*, which purports to present 'the twelue priuate

*Fig. 4: Monument (1627) to Anne Keighley (d.1598), Ault Hucknall, Nottinghamshire (detail). Photo: Norman Hammond*

morale vertues, as Aristotle hath deuised'.[9] As is the case with Anne Keighley, there are no portraits of the deceased on this monument – the brothers are represented by the tutelary deities of the Military and Civil lives – Mars and Minerva – by their empty armour (Henry) and peer's robes (William), which encapsulate the public roles by which they were known, and by a skeleton and a shrouded corpse (what they have become).

The choice of an individual monument for Anne Keighley in a church different from that of her husband (Ault Hucknall is the church for Hardwick; Edensor for Chatsworth) serves (as was the case with Cecily Sandys) to emphasise that the couple are separated in death: there is no hope of the joyful post-resurrection reunion present in so many marital monuments – something which may even embrace more than one spouse, as on the earl of Donegal's 1650 monument at Eggesford, Devon, to his 'two Deare and unparaled Wives', or that to Thomas Alleyn (d.1650) at Great Witchingham, Norfolk – 'Death here advantage hath of life I spye, One husband with two wives at once may lye'. The person excluded from all this is, of course, the first earl of Devonshire's second wife, mother of Sir John – she has no monument. By memorialising his father and mother in this way the second earl of Devonshire held them up as a paragons of virtue and as members of a distinguished family (the first earl shares a double monument with his brother, not – as might have been expected – with his wife) and neatly wipes his stepmother out of the memorialised record.

There is no reason to suppose that family tension lies behind the Sandys monument: as eldest son Sir Samuel was the correct person to erect such a memorial, and he seems to have remained on good terms with his siblings. It is perhaps a tribute to Cecily Sandys herself that her eldest son wished to commemorate her as a distinct person, rather than let her only monumental representation be as his father's wife. Nor is there necessarily any family tension in the last, but most extraordinary, monument with which this paper deals: that to Lady Deane (d.1633) at Great Maplestead, Essex.

In the seventeenth century the south transept of Great Maplestead church was turned into a funerary chapel for the Deane family. To the east is the monument to Sir John Deane (d.1625), erected by his wife in 1628. This, despite its attribution to William Wright,[10] is of mixed quality: the figures of the widow and children who kneel along the top are accomplished, but that of Sir John himself is comparatively crude (Fig. 5). There is a conventional Latin inscription in the dexter panel:

*Fig. 5: Monument (1628) attributed to William Wright, to Sir John Deane (d.1625), Great Maplestead, Essex. Photo: Norman Hammond*

MEMORIÆ SACRVM
IOHANNIS DEANE EQVITIS AVRATI EQVITATIS IN AGRO
ESSEXIENSE PROPRÆFECTI
QVEM
MORIBVS SVAVISSIMVS INTEGERRIMISQ:
ANNVM ÆTATIS 45 AGENTE
D.O.M.
IPSIVS SATISFACIENS, POPVLARIV MILITVM SED MAXIME, ANNÆ
VXORIS PROLISQ: NVMEROSI VOTIS ADEMIT:
ANNA VXOR MŒSTISSIMA CVM PVBLICO BONORV LVCTV,
PRIVATOQ: TOTIVS STEMMATIS MŒRORE
POSVIT
A.D. 1628

(*Translation*: Sacred to the memory of Sir John Deane, Knt., Deputy Lieutenant of the County of Essex. Whom being a man of most agreeable manners and upright conduct and in the forty-fifth year of his age the supremely good and great Deity in his pleasure took away from the prayers of his [train bands], but especially from those of his wife, Anna, and numerous friends. Anna, his most sorrowing wife, buried him in the year of our Lord 1628, with the public lamentation of good men and the private grief of the whole family)[11]

The sinister panel, which must have been left blank in preparation for Lady Deane's own epitaph, now contains an inscription lavishly praising Sir John which was added by his daughter, presumably after Lady Deane was given her own monument:

LETT POSTERITY KNOW

S[R]: IOHN DEANE OF DINES HALL, IN GREAT MAPPLESTED
IN Y[E] COVNT[Y] OF ESSEX KN[T]; ONE OF Y[E] DEPVT[Y] LIEVTENANT[S]
& IVSTICES OF PEACE IN Y[E] SAME SHYRE, WHO WAS
DESCENDED FROM Y[E] WORTHY FAMILY OF Y[E]: DEANES
OF LANCASH[E]: & WHO MATCHT W[TH] M[RS] ANNE DRVRY
OF Y[E] HONO[R] TRIBE OF Y[E] DRVRIES OF RIDDLEW[TH]
IN NORFOLKE BY WHŌ HE HAD 6 DAVGHT[RS]
& 2 SONNES DYED ON Y[E] 17 DAY OF
FEBR:[RE] IN Y[E] YEARE OF HIS LIFE 43
IN Y[E] YEARE OF GRACE 1625.

HIS PARTES & PERSON WERE ADMIRABLE, DESARTE & HEE WERE TWYNNS: HIS PIETYE WAS Y[E] FOVNTAINE OF HIS ACTIONS & HIS HEARTE WAS Y[E] SEATE OF EQVITYE: TRVTH WAS Y[E] BEST INTER PRETOVR OF HIS WORKS: HIS MEDITATIONS WERE WHOLY BOVNDE IN HEAVEN: HIS CHARITYE ASKED TYME TO GIVE & GAVE NO TYME TO ASKING: Y[E] PLEASVRES OF HIS LIFE WERE Y[E] PASSAGES OF VIRTVE DEATH WAS HIS TRIVMPHE NOT HIS CONQVEROVR: HE WAS BVRIED IN Y[E] TEARES OF Y[E] FAITHVLL, & SHALL RISE IN Y[E] IOY OF Y[E] RIGHTEOVS.

To whose perpetuall memory
Anne Deane his eldest daught[r]
did make & dedicate this Inscriptiõ.

Facing Sir John's monument across the chapel, so that it also faces east, is the monument to his widow, who died in 1633. It was erected in 1634, and is the work of William Wright.[12] It shows her son, Sir Dru Deane, lying on the tomb chest in armour on a straw mat, his hands crossed on his breast, while behind him under a coffered arch, the shrouded figure of his mother steps forward on a 'vase-shaped pedestal',[13] her sinister hand raised in a gesture of wonder, her eyes open, looking up towards the underside of the arch which is carved with a representation of heaven, including angels blowing trumpets (Fig. 6a). The centre of the arch is interrupted, and in the gap is a heavenly crown, which two further angels seated above the arch hand down to Lady Deane (Fig. 6b). Sir Dru cannot see this with his earthly eyes, as it is behind him – this is Sir Dru's vision of his mother's reception into Heaven.

The inscription goes far beyond those already examined proclaiming the mother's virtues:

LET ALL TIME REMEMBER

Y$^E$ WORTHYNES OF Y$^E$

LADY DEANE

WHO LIVED Y$^E$ FAITHFVLL

WIFE & DIED Y$^E$ CONSTANT

WIDDOW OF S$^R$ IOHN DEANE

OF MAPPLESTED IN Y$^E$

COVNTY OF ESSEX

KNIGHT

LET NO SORROWE FORGET

THAT SHE DEPARTED THIS

LIFE ON Y$^E$ 25$^{TH}$ OF MAY

1633 OF WHOM

TRVTH TESTIFIES

| | |
|---|---|
| HER SHAPE WAS RARE | HER BEAVTY EXQVISITE |
| HER WYTT ACCVRATE | HER IVDGM$^T$ SINGVLAR |
| HER ENTERTAYM$^T$ HARTY | HER CONVERSATIÕ LOVELY |
| HER HARTE MERCIFVL | HER HAND HELPFVLL |
| HER COVRSES MODEST | HER DISCOVRSES WISE |
| HER CHARITY HEAVENLY | HER AMITY CONSTANT |
| HER PRACTISE HOLY | HER RELIGION PVRE |
| HER VOWES LAWFVLL | HER MEDITATIONS DIVINE |
| HER FAYTH VNFAYGND | HER HOPE STABLE |
| HER PRAYERS DEVOVT | HER DEVOTIONS DIVRNALL |
| HER DAYES SHORT | HER LIFE EVERLASTING |

TO WHOSE BELOVED MEMORY S$^R$.

DRV DEANE HER ELDEST SONNE

HERE PROSTRATE AT HER

FEET ERECTS THIS

MONVMENT

APRIL Y$^E$ 14 1634

The inscription, as much as the design, trumps her husband's in every way: Posterity must remember his virtues, all time Lady Deane's (it is worth noting that this monument post-dates the *First Folio* of Shakespeare in 1623, which includes Ben Jonson's claim that 'he was not of an age, but for all time'). Sir John has the virtues expected of a gentleman; Lady Deane excels in every

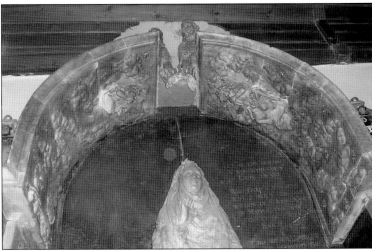

*Fig. 6a (top): Monument (1634) by William Wright to Lady Deane (d.1633), Great Maplestead, Essex. Photo: Norman Hammond*

*Fig. 6b (bottom): Great Maplestead, Essex, detail of the monument shown in Figure 6a. Photo: Norman Hammond*

aspect of her being, face and figure as well as virtue and intellect. The monument itself has a double-inscription panel of which the inscription occupies only half, and it seems likely that Sir Dru intended to be buried with his mother, with his funerary inscription occupying what is now a blank space.

Like Cecily Sandys's, Lady Deane's monument arrogates the imagery of the BVM: the apotheosis of Lady Deane, with the vault of the arch/vault of heaven breaking open to receive her as she receives her eternal crown, has irresistible parallels with conventional representations of the Assumption of the Virgin, as she is received into Heaven and crowned by her Son. Even the shroud has echoes of the long robes in which the Virgin is conventionally depicted. The Catholic imagery of the Virgin and Child was used well into the Reformation in commemorating women who had died in childbirth, as at Egham, Surrey, on the monument to the two wives of Sir John Denham (d.1612 and 1628), and Evesbatch, Herefordshire on the monument to Margaret Dobyns (d.1658).[14] Even for older women the imagery of the BVM still provides a source for the depiction of the ideal woman, to which men turn when they wish to honour and commemorate their mothers.

## Acknowledgments

*I am grateful to Professor E. J. Kenney, FBA for checking my Latin translations, to Dr Anna Abulafia for discussing with me the uses of the imagery of the Blessed Virgin Mary and Professor Norman Hammond, FBA for taking the photographs. Other debts are acknowledged individually.*

### Notes

1 Southwell had an archiepiscopal palace for the see of York; four medieval archbishops are buried there, but no other post-Reformation archbishop.

2 Dr Jane Renfrew has confirmed my identification of the plant. Dr Anna Abulafia has suggested to me that there may be a reminiscence in the open blossoms on their stems curling round the uprights of the arbour of the *rosa sine spina* associated with the BVM and also of the flowering rods of Aaron (Numbers xvii. 6–8) – the symbol of true priesthood, appropriate to an archbishop's widow – and Jesse (Isaiah xi. 1), again associated with the BVM.

3 P. Muilman, *A New and Complete History of Essex … By a Gentleman*, 6 vols. (1769–72), I, 201. Muilman additionally claims that the pillars are surmounted by figures of phoenixes. It is not clear whether the monument has been altered since Muilman saw it, or whether he misdescribed it. He is inaccurate about the detail of other monuments.

4 The species shown on the monument could be *Clematis viticella*, introduced from Europe about 1569.

5 See J. Wilson, 'Go for Baroque: the Bruce mausoleum at Maulden, Bedfordshire', *Church Monuments* 22 (2007), 66–95 (p.79).

6 See L. Stone, *The Crisis of the Aristocracy* 1558–1641 (Oxford, corrected ed. 1979), 590–92, 645–49; L. Stone, *The Family, Sex and Marriage in England 1500–1800* (New York, 1977), 105–114.

7   B. Burke, *A Genealogical History of the Dormant, Abeyant, Forfeited, and Extinct Peerages of the British Empire* (1883), 427b. The required Dukedom was created in 1715 for Gervase's nephew Evelyn, third son of his elder brother William, who had succeeded his father and two older brothers as earl of Kingston.

8   The virtues seem to have been moved: reading from the viewer's left along the sarcophagus lid they are now Prudence (with a laurel-wreathed helmet, holding a snake – a symbol of wisdom, as in Matthew x. 16, 'Be ye therefore wise as serpents'); Obedience (wearing a slave-collar); Chastity (veiled, to show that she avoids unbecoming sights, and holding a lamb, symbol of innocence); Piety (holding what is possibly the remains of a cross-shaft); and Love/Charity (with a cornucopia).

9   'A Letter of the Authors ... to ... Sir Walter Raleigh', annexed to *The Faerie Queene* (1590) (Edmund Spenser, *Poems*, ed. E. de Selincourt, (1912), 407–08 (p. 407)).

10  J. Bettley and N. Pevsner: *The Buildings of England: Essex* (New Haven and London, 2007), 414. The attribution depends on the documentation of the monument to Lady Deane.

11  This is the translation from F. Chancellor, *The ancient sepulchral monuments of Essex* (London, 1890), 298, but there are problems with the inscription as now existing and with Chancellor's translation: Professor E. J. Kenney, to whom I am indebted for the information that 'populares milites' are train bands, informs me that 'either the inscription has been garbled in recopying or its composer was a very indifferent Latinist'. I am, as always, profoundly grateful to to Professor Kenney for his help.

12  A. White, *A Biographical Dictionary of London Tomb Sculptors c. 1560–c. 1660*, Walpole Society, vol. 61 (1999), 145–46.

13  F. Chancellor, *The Ancient Sepulchral Monuments of Essex* (1890), 299.

14  J. Wilson, 'Dead Fruit: the commemoration of still-born and unbaptized children in Early Modern England', *Church Monuments* 17 (2002), 89–106 (p.91).

# Private act or public commemoration? The Yorke family and the eighteenth-century church monument

*Kerry Bristol*

*Kerry Bristol is a senior lecturer in the history of architecture at the University of Leeds and co-editor of* Church Monuments.

THIS PAPER EXPLORES church monuments associated with the Yorke family of Wimpole Hall, Cambridgeshire. Rather than treat these works as the unique output of an artist, however, the concern will be with the patrons. By examining who commissioned these monuments and the factors that influenced their location, it will be seen that certain monuments were intended to 'speak' to each other. An examination of the inscriptions can also tell us much about those commemorated, and those commemorating, in eighteenth-century Britain.

## The Yorke family

Because the Yorke family was large and tightly knit, introducing key figures will aid in understanding their cousins and connections and, thus, the monuments under discussion here.

At the head of the family stood Philip Yorke (1690–1764), Lord Chancellor during the Walpole and Newcastle administrations. Yorke was born into a legal family from Dover and had been destined for the law from an early age.[1] He was educated at Bethnal Green, Middlesex before leaving to become an articled clerk to a London attorney. Yorke entered the Middle Temple in 1708; was called to the Bar in 1714; elected MP for Lewes in 1719; appointed Solicitor-General and given a knighthood in 1720; made Attorney-General in 1724; Lord Chief Justice of the King's Bench, Baron Hardwicke, and member of the Privy Council in 1733; and promoted to Lord Chancellor in 1737. His final reward was to be created earl of Hardwicke in 1754. He stepped down as Lord Chancellor in 1756, although continued as a member of the Privy Council for another four years and died a very wealthy man in 1764.

As befitted Hardwicke's devotion to the law, he married Margaret Cocks (*c.*1695–1761), the niece of John Somers, Lord Chancellor to William III. Seven of their children survived to maturity. Philip (known as Viscount Royston) and Charles are of concern here because they commissioned the first family monuments.

Philip Yorke (1720–90) benefitted from his father's meteoric rise.[2] He trained for the law and matriculated from Corpus Christi College, Cambridge, in 1737, receiving within a year the sinecure of Teller of the Exchequer. From 1741–7 he was MP for Reigate, Surrey and was thereafter member for Cambridgeshire until he inherited the earldom and became High Steward of Cambridge

University in succession to his father. He was also Lord Lieutenant of the county 1757–90.

Royston married Jemima Campbell, in 1740, a fortnight before she inherited the Marquisate de Grey and Wrest Park, Bedfordshire from her grandfather, the Duke of Kent. Unusually for married couples of this era, they supported two distinct patrimonies because the Duke's will had stipulated that the contents of Wrest Park were to remain in trust in the house as heirlooms.[3]

The career of Charles Yorke (1722–70) was as carefully laid out as that of his elder brother and he received a similar education, the difference being that Charles was expected to practice law as well as study it.[4] He was called to the Bar in 1746, became MP for Reigate when Royston vacated the seat, was appointed Solicitor-General to the Prince of Wales in 1754 and Solicitor-General in 1756. Unfortunately he was not the politician his father had been. Yorke aspired to the post of Attorney-General in 1757, was successful in 1762 but resigned when pressured by the Duke of Newcastle and was in and out of office thereafter. The Great Seal and a peerage remained elusive until 17 January 1770. By that point, however, Yorke's health had been undermined. He died three days later.

## The Church of St Andrew, Wimpole, Cambridgeshire

The site that the Yorkes chose as the location for the first of their monuments was the parish church of St Andrew adjacent to Wimpole Hall, the estate that Lord Hardwicke had purchased in 1740. A previous owner had restored the medieval church in 1732 but Lord Hardwicke razed the old building and erected a Georgian preaching box in its place. The only part of the earlier building to survive was the Chicheley chapel (named after the family who had owned Wimpole 1428–1686). The church was regothicised in 1887, when the chapel was opened to the main body of the church,[5] spoiling the effect that the Yorkes had created.

The first of the Yorke monuments was to Catharine Freman (1737–59), Charles Yorke's first wife (Fig. 1). Designed by James Stuart and executed by Peter Scheemakers, it was erected on the north wall of the Chicheley chapel.

As Ingrid Roscoe has remarked, the 'asymmetrical arrangement and the naturalism of the boys and foliate ornaments give the work a rococo feeling'.[6] It is a pretty monument, but one somehow at odds with Scheemakers' reputation as a practitioner in the classical tradition and with the years that Stuart had spent in Italy and Greece. But were the Yorkes concerned with cutting edge style? Lord Hardwicke and his eldest son were bibliophiles,

*Fig. 1: James Stuart and Peter Scheemakers, monument to Catharine Freman, first wife of Charles Yorke, at St Andrew, Wimpole, Cambridgeshire, 1761–2. Photo: Conway Library, Courtauld Institute of Art*

but, beyond amassing a collection of portraits, the only member of the family with any genuine feeling for the arts was Elizabeth Anson and she died in 1760, too early to have played any part in this commission. The monument to Catharine Freman is not about 'style'. Instead, her importance to the Yorkes was twofold:

HERE LIE THE REMAINS OF CATHARINE, DAUGHTER
AND SOLE HEIR OF WILLIAM FREMAN ESQ[R] OF HAMELS
IN HERTFORDSHIRE BY CATHARINE, DAUGHTER OF
SIR THOMAS POPE BLOUNT BAR[T] OF TITTENHANGER
IN THE SAME COUNTY. SHE WAS MARRIED MAY XIX,
MDCCLV TO THE HON[BLE] CHARLES YORKE, SECOND SON
OF PHILIP EARL OF HARDWICKE, SOLICITOR GENERAL
TO KING GEORGE THE SECOND, AND ATTORNEY
GENERAL TO KING GEORGE THE THIRD; BY WHOM SHE
HAD THREE CHILDREN; TWO DAUGHTERS, MARGARET
AND CATHARINA, WHO DIED BEFORE HER; AND ONE
SON PHILIP, NOW LIVING. SHE DIED OF A MALIGNANT
FEVER, JULY X, MDCCLIX, AGED TWENTY TWO YEARS.

TO THE GRACES OF HER PERSON SHE ADDED THE
JUSTEST SENSE OF THINGS AND THE MOST ARTLESS AND
ENGAGING MANNER. THESE GAINED HER THE ESTEEM
OF THE WORLD: WHILST THE GENEROUS AFFECTIONS
OF HER HEART, HER AMIABLE TEMPER AND A
CONSTANT CHEARFULNESS (THE HAPPY RESULT OF
INNOCENCE, PIETY, AND VIRTUE) ENDEARED HER TO
ALL WHO KNEW HER MOST INTIMATELY, HER FAMILY,
HER FRIENDS AND HER HUSBAND, WHO HAS CAUSED
THIS MONUMENT TO BE ERECTED, IN TENDER AND
AFFECTIONATE REGARD TO HER MEMORY.

At the time of her death, Catharine Freman was heiress to two Hertfordshire estates, one through her father William and one through her mother Catharina. Both estates eventually passed to her son Philip. Had Philly (as he was known) been born female, he would still have inherited Hamels and Tyttenhanger, but it was the gender of her surviving child that had dictated where Catharine Freman was buried. In 1759, Philly was heir-apparent to the much larger Wimpole estate. The Yorke/Greys had two daughters and the absence of a son meant that their eldest daughter would inherit Wrest and the Grey title, while Wimpole and the Hardwicke title would pass to a nephew on the Yorke side of the family. This is indeed what happened in 1790, when Philly became third earl of Hardwicke. That the first earl paid for the monument also suggests that some dynastic statement was intended.[7]

Many eighteenth-century inscriptions relating to women referred to virtue, piety and the almost Rousseau-like naturalness of their emotions, but Charles Yorke sincerely regretted the loss of his wife and some of what he chose to record for posterity was true. Catharine Freman was much loved by the Yorkes, who were deeply shocked by her death from what was probably diptheria. In his response to a letter of condolence from Ralph Freman, Yorke referred to his marriage as 'the greatest blessing of my whole Life' before resigning himself to the will of God. Confessing that he '[spoke] without reserve the sense of my heart', what followed was disconcertingly like a rough draft of his wife's epitaph.[8]

The second monument erected at Wimpole – that to the first earl and countess of Hardwicke – is the most renowned of the Stuart/Scheemakers partnership (Fig. 2). Thanks to surviving correspondence between Viscount Royston (now the second earl) and Daniel Wray and between James Stuart and Thomas Anson, it is also the best documented.[9]

The earl had requested that he be buried 'privately and without Pomp in the vault adjoining to the Parish Church of Wimpole' with a memorial that was 'decent but not magnificent, and the inscription modest'.[10] After careful negotiation with Stuart and Scheemakers, the second earl agreed a design that included figures of Minerva and Pudicitia (the 'matronal Virtue'), a sarcophagus and portrait medallions.[11] The Hardwicke monument bears more of Stuart's classical rigour than that of its sculptor, but allegorical figures standing to either side of an image of the deceased were hardly new in the 1760s. They usually represented the virtues or religious beliefs of the commemorated, as they do here, although an interesting aspect of this monument is the sculptural equality accorded the couple; the medallions are of equal size and one figure apiece 'speaks' for their respective qualities.

More monuments to lawyers were erected in the early- to mid-eighteenth century than ever before, perhaps linked to a rise in esteem for the law as a profession.[12] Members of the professions (especially law, medicine and the church) were better educated than many men of business and thus formed a key link between the traditional landed elite and men of business in the rise of polite society. As Lord Hardwicke's career demonstrates, the law was an excellent path to preferment. Prestigious location of a monument was a sign of power and status. This being the case, why did Royston respect his father's wishes and erect a monument to his parents in a tiny rural church instead of Westminster Abbey, which would seem a more suitable place for commemoration of a high-profile public figure?

*Fig. 2: James Stuart and Peter Scheemakers, monument to Philip Yorke, first earl of Hardwicke, and Margaret Cocks, countess of Hardwicke, at St Andrew, Wimpole, Cambridgeshire, 1764–6. Photo: Conway Library, Courtauld Institute of Art*

Any monument represents a certain investment in space[13] – and critics delighted in repeating stories of the parsimonious Yorkes[14] – but cost is unlikely to have been a factor here because any additional expenditure associated with situating a monument in the Abbey would have been offset by the cost of shipping the finished monument to Wimpole.

Since monuments to less worthy men and women had been erected in the Abbey, was the second earl deterred by the disgust felt by many that political corruption had rendered fame debased? As Craske so ably demonstrates, the traditional landed elite frequently withdrew to their country estates and erected monuments stressing their disinterest in political faction and preferment when faced with the juggernaut of Robert Walpole's regime.[15] The Yorkes were 'new money', new to the landed classes, and only recently elevated to the peerage, however, and, as Whigs loyal to the Hanoverian dynasty, and seldom in Opposition, they had no need to create a myth of virtuous retreat to the countryside. Indeed, the proximity of Wimpole to Cambridge negated any true notion of retreat. Charles Yorke even represented the university in parliament from 1768–70. Although it is unlikely that the proportion of 'public' business conducted at Wimpole versus that conducted elsewhere can ever be known, the monuments at Wimpole were hardly invisible. In erecting a monument to his parents at Wimpole, Royston was marking the foundation of a dynasty. As the monument was only quasi-private, even the inscription was carefully worded to stress Lord Hardwicke's public status (not mere wealth) and his personal qualities, as well as the fecundity of his wife.

As the Chicheley chapel was to be the Yorkes' collective resting place, the next monument to be erected was that to Charles Yorke, who had accepted the Great Seal against his family's wishes. The result had been a violent quarrel with his brother (if Charles was irresolute, Philip was irascible) and Yorke died soon after. Pernicious gossip suggested it was suicide although the symptoms suggest haemorrhaging from a peptic ulcer.[16] The second earl turned to Scheemakers for a monument similar in size to that of Catharine Freman (Fig. 3). That Stuart was not involved with this monument suggests that style was only a secondary concern in favour of recording Yorke's self-sacrificing patriotism and disinterested public service. The inscription even records that 'The Great Seal was delivered to him Jan.$^{\text{y}}$ 17.$^{\text{th}}$ 1770, at a juncture very unfavourable for his accepting it' when the reality was rather different; his brothers had not wanted him to become lord chancellor in the Grafton administration.

The second earl died in 1790 and is commemorated by a monument (Fig. 4) that stresses his preference for a quiet,

*Fig. 3: Peter Scheemakers, monument to Charles Yorke, at St Andrew, Wimpole, Cambridgeshire, 1770.*

contemplative life to one of naked ambition or active service (in fact, he was a hypochondriac who turned down office on the grounds of ill health). Joseph (1724–92) and John (1728–1801) and their respective wives (Figs. 5 & 6) soon followed. James is the only Yorke brother missing (he lived at his wife's Gloucestershire estate), although his children Charles and Mary came 'home' to Wimpole. There are also monuments to the third earl, his wife and sons, and to the fourth earl in the Chicheley Chapel and to Charles Yorke's second wife and their son and daughter-in-law in the chancel.

As this roll call demonstrates, a woman's (posthumous) place was by her husband's side in Georgian England and the Yorke sisters played no role in the history carefully constructed by their brothers at Wimpole. Elizabeth Anson and Margaret Heathcote were buried with their husbands. The anomaly is Jemima de Grey.

*Fig. 4: Thomas Banks, monument to Philip Yorke, second earl of Hardwicke (d.1790), at St Andrew, Wimpole, Cambridgeshire.*

She was separated from her husband in death as she had never been in life and her monument takes its place with those to the rest of the Greys at Flitton, Bedfordshire. Touchingly, she erected a monument to her husband in the same mausoleum.

## Hamels, Hertfordshire, and the Freman family

Hamels was a small estate situated near the village of Braughing. It first appears as a separate estate in 1580 when John Brograve, attorney for the duchy of Lancaster under Elizabeth and James I, bought the land.[17] Hamels then passed by descent until 1707, when it was sold to pay the creditors of Sir Thomas Brograve.[18]

Among Brograve's creditors was Ralph Freman (1666–1742), whose father owned nearby Aspenden Hall. The Fremans were minor gentry resident at Aspenden since *c*.1610, although Ralph Freman had lived at Ecton, Northamptonshire since 1699, when

*Fig.5: John Bacon, monument to Joseph Yorke, at St Andrew, Wimpole, Cambridgeshire, 1798.*

his wife Elizabeth had inherited her family estate. Ecton was sold and the money put towards the acquisition of Hamels in 1713.[19]

Ralph and Elizabeth Freman had six children, three daughters and three sons (twins William and Catesby, b.1702 and Ralph, b.1706). Presumably they intended to treat Hamels as a secondary estate, suitable for Catesby when William inherited Aspenden. Ralph entered the church and was evidently not to be provided for in this manner. Ralph Freman died in 1742 (the same year as the unmarried Catesby) and his widow continued to live at Aspenden until her death.[20] Curiously, William resided at Hamels until his marriage in 1731 to Catharina Blount, when the couple moved to Aspenden to live with his parents. They returned to Hamels in 1745 and, thereafter, Hamels became the main family seat.[21]

William and Catharina Freman had one daughter, Catharine, who married Charles Yorke. William died in 1749, when the manors passed to his brother, Revd Dr Ralph Freeman, Prebendary of Salisbury.[22] Surviving correspondence reveals that Ralph Freman, D.D., had officiated at the wedding of his niece to Charles Yorke and that the two families were very close.[23]

Freman was a tidy businessman who had settled most of his affairs before his death. Apart from a few small legacies, he left everything to his great-nephew Philly Yorke, then a boy of fifteen.

*Fig. 6: Richard Westmacott the elder, monument to John Yorke (d.1801), at St Andrew, Wimpole, Cambridgeshire.*

*Fig. 6: Richard Westmacott the elder, monument to John Yorke (d.1801), at St Andrew, Wimpole, Cambridgeshire.*

His will then stipulated that, should Philly:

> happen to die without lawful Issue before he shall attain his Age of One and Twenty years, Then I Give devise and bequeath all and every my said Real and Personal Estates whatsoever and wheresoever unto his Uncle the Right Honorable the Earl of Hardwicke his heirs Executors Administrators and Assigns.[24]

The monument that Lord Hardwicke commissioned from James Stuart and Peter Scheemakers' son Thomas is characteristic of their partnership in the 1770s (Fig. 7). Its 'combination of a massive sarcophagus, portrait medallions and coarsely sculpted boys, executed in showy polychrome marbles'[25] can also be seen in the Cocks monuments discussed below, but it is not style that is pertinent here. As with the monuments at Wimpole, location matters. Lord Hardwicke chose St Mary, Braughing, instead of St Mary, Aspenden.[26]

St Mary, Braughing, dates mainly from the thirteenth and fifteenth centuries. Restoration in 1888 removed most of the Georgian interventions,[27] and today two monuments dominate the chancel. That on the north side commemorates John Brograve (d.1625) and his younger brother Charles (d.1602); that on the south side is complicated by both the inscription and the presence of medallions set into the wall on either side. Lord Hardwicke

*Fig. 7: James Stuart and Thomas Scheemakers, monument to Ralph and Agnes, William and Catharina, and Ralph and Elizabeth Freman, at St Mary, Braughing, Hertfordshire.*

commemorated Ralph and Agnes, William and Catharina, and Ralph and Elizabeth because they were the last of the Fremans to live at Hamels. This monument speaks of a family that died out in the male line and the legal transmission of their property. The Fremans take their place opposite the Brograves as former owners, which may also explain why their monuments are of comparable size.

## The Cocks family of Eastnor, Herefordshire

The Cocks family have been the subject of surprisingly little research, possibly because the survival rate of their papers is not high, but more likely because their most illustrious forebear was not a Cocks at all; he was Sir John Somers, created first Baron Somers of Evesham, Worcestershire in 1697, Lord Chancellor to William III. There are also so many Cockses that they are a genealogical horror story.[28]

Richard Cocks purchased the manor of Castleditch, Herefordshire early in the reign of James I.[29] He and his wife had two sons, Thomas and Richard. Thomas, in turn, had three sons, Charles, John, and (Revd) Thomas. Charles married Mary Somers, the sister and co-heir of Lord Chancellor Somers. They lived at Worcester and raised five children including Margaret, who married Philip Yorke, and John, who married his cousin Mary, the daughter of Revd Thomas Cocks and sole heir to the Castleditch estate. Mary and John Cocks had twelve children, including Charles (1725–1806), Elizabeth (b.1729) and Joseph (1733–75).

Surviving letters attest to the close bonds of kinship and friendship between Charles Cocks and his Yorke cousins. The correspondence is frequently concerned with political matters – unsurprising given that Reigate returned two MPs to the House of Commons, one a Cocks and the other a Yorke, for most of the eighteenth century[30] – but personal affairs were also discussed. There were requests for patronage of various dependents, congratulations on betrothals and marriages, news of illnesses and bereavements, and even an obsequious letter asking Philip Yorke to change banks from Hoare's to Cocks and Biddulph (founded by Charles Cocks' brothers Thomas and James).[31] This makes it all the more disappointing that there is no documentary evidence to support an exploration of the two monuments designed by James Stuart and executed by Thomas Scheemakers in St John the Baptist, Eastnor.

With the exception of the fourteenth-century west tower, the church of St John the Baptist was almost entirely rebuilt in 1852.[32] The monuments, both commissioned by Elizabeth Cocks, appear to be in their original location, impossibly cramped under the tower (Figs. 8 & 9). The monument to Joseph Cocks commemorates a favourite brother whose virtues would otherwise be lost to posterity but the inscription is cryptic:

No Man ever pofsefsed clearer Principles of Religion and Virtue, or acted upon Them with greater Steadinefs. Blest with a sweet and most affectionate Temper, He discharged with Ease to Himself every Duty incumbent upon the Son, Husband Father and Friend. Thus exact in his private Life. He was not without the Ambition of distinguishing Himself in a public station. The Friendly Heart is generally disposed to be Sociable in a wider Sphere. This was his Case very remarkably. He was a Lover of the Constitution of his Country, and had studied it with Care in its earliest and best Expositors, Being thus trained by deep study, and close Application to the Knowledge of Constitutional and Legal Liberty, He was prepared to have stood forth its bold and determined Advocate; But Divine Providence seemed to think a degenerate Age unworthy of such an Example. He was taken away from the Evil to come – Being weaned from the World by some Disapointments and particularly so by a great private Lofs in his own Family.

The critical year appears to have been 1766, when a letter from Charles Yorke to Charles Cocks suggests that the 'Disapointment' had been the loss of a lucrative government post.[33] Charles Cocks' reply has also survived:

121

I am very sorry for my brothers loss, which is of serious consequence to him, tho' I do'nt [*sic*] well see how it could have been avoided; My Father, it is true, may, if he pleases, easily repair it and I shall heartily recommend it to him so to do, especially as he is so very deserving of his encouragement, from the extraordinary care he has taken of his estates, and other affairs in which he has been employed by him, and for which he has hitherto received little or no compensation.[34]

A further letter from Charles Yorke enquires if John Cocks had agreed to help his son,[35] and two from Charles Cocks reveal that the family were now looking to their Yorke cousins for help because the answer had been a stark refusal. The 'disposition, which is all in the present case, [was] entirely wanting',[36] and Joseph was faced with severe financial hardship. And there the trail goes cold. Presumably unable to find political preferment – to be the 'bold and determined Advocate' of 'Constitutional and Legal Liberty' described on his memorial – he died a broken man, much mourned by his spinster sister Elizabeth, who appears to have looked after the interests of his children. One wonders how the rest of the family responded to this ever-present reminder of failure in their midst?

*Fig. 9: James Stuart and Thomas Scheemakers, monument to Mary Cocks (d.1779), at St John the Baptist, Eastnor, Herefordshire.*

No such mystery lies behind the monument to Mary Cocks. Elizabeth Cocks was the executrix and residuary legatee of her mother's estate, as well as one of three trustees appointed to administer it.[37] This must be why she, and not her eldest brother, erected the monument. Twenty years earlier, the inscription would almost certainly have made mention of this inheritance and recorded that Mary Cocks had brought the Eastnor estate to her marriage, but Elizabeth Cocks did not express gratitude. Instead, her concern was to depict Mary as a paragon of 'natural' motherhood who taught her children to read, led by Christian example, and was never idle, in spite of the 'difsipated and extravagant Age' in which she lived. Here we have a monument intended to act as an exemplar for future generations of the Cocks family, nestled firmly in its bosom in rural Herefordshire.

## Conclusion

In the final analysis, when the extended Yorke family turned to the Stuart/Scheemakers partnership for a church monument, they did so because they wanted a time-honoured theme, or a minor variation thereof. The resulting monuments were very good but it is the human stories that lie behind them that explain their existence and make them so interesting.

*All photographs are by the author unless otherwise stated.*

**Notes**

1  *Oxford Dictionary of National Biography (ODNB)*, (eds. H. C. G. Matthew and B. Harrison), 60 vols. (Oxford, 2004), 60, 847–51; R. Sedgwick, *The History of Parliament: The House of Commons 1715–1754*, 2 vols. (1985), 2, 569–70.

2  *ODNB*, 60, 851–52; Sedgwick, *House of Commons*, 2, 570–71; L. Namier and J. Brooke, *The History of Parliament: The House of Commons 1754–1790*, 3 vols. (1985), 3, 683–85.

3  Bedfordshire and Luton Archives and Records Service, Lucas Manuscript L 32/11–13. See also Lucas Manuscript L32/40–41.

4  *ODNB*, 60, 831–3; Sedgwick, *House of Commons*, 2, 568; Namier and Brooke, *House of Commons*, 3, 675–78.

5  D. Souden, *Wimpole Hall, Cambridgeshire* (1991), 85.

6  I. Roscoe, 'Peter Scheemakers, business conduct and workshop practice with Catalogue Raisonné', *Walpole Society*, 61 (1999), 163–304 (pp. 242–43).

7  I. Roscoe, 'James "Athenian" Stuart and the Scheemakers family: a lucrative partnership between architect and sculptors', *Apollo*, 126 (September 1987), 178–84, (p. 184); Roscoe, 'Business conduct and workshop practice', 242–43.

8  Hertfordshire Archives and Local Studies Centre (HALSC), D/End F50.

9  Roscoe, 'James "Athenian" Stuart', 181; K. Bristol, 'James "Athenian" Stuart (1713–1788) and the genesis of the Greek Revival in English architecture', (doctoral thesis, Courtauld Institute of Art, 1997), 364–69; M. G. Sullivan, 'Stuart and the changing relationship between architects and sculptors in eighteenth-century Britain', in S. Weber Soros (ed.), *James 'Athenian' Stuart: The Rediscovery of Antiquity* (London, New Haven and New York, 2006), 384–411 (pp. 390–94); Roscoe, 'Business conduct and workshop practice', 243–45.

10  British Library (BL), Add. MS 36,229, fol.128; Roscoe, 'James "Athenian" Stuart', 181; Souden, *Wimpole Hall*, 26.

11  Staffordshire County Record Office, Lichfield Manuscript D615/P(S)/1/6/7–8, 10, 12. See also Roscoe, 'James "Athenian" Stuart', 181–82.

12 M. Craske, *The Silent Rhetoric of the Body: A History of Monumental Sculpture and Commemorative Art in England, 1720–1770* (New Haven and London, 2007), 387.

13 N. Llewellyn, *The Art of Death. Visual Culture in the English Death Ritual c.1500–c.1800* (1991), 105.

14 Souden, *Wimpole Hall*, 22.

15 Craske, *Silent Rhetoric*, 6–27.

16 J. Godber, 'The Life of the Marchioness Grey of Wrest Park, 1722–97', *Bedfordshire Historical Record Society*, 47 (1968), 7–123 (p. 85).

17 *The Victoria History of the Counties of England (VCH): Hertfordshire*, 4 vols. (Folkestone and London, 1912), 3, 313. See also D. R. Smith, *The Story of Braughing* (Braughing, 1971), 12 and A. Rowe (ed.), *Garden Making and the Freman Family: A Memoir of Hamels, 1713–1733*, Hertfordshire Record Publications, 17 (Hertford, 2001), xxxv.

18 *VCH: Hertfordshire*, 3, 314; Rowe, *Garden Making*, xi–xiii.

19 Rowe, *Garden Making*, xx.

20 Rowe, *Garden Making*, xlii.

21 Rowe, *Garden Making*, xlii, 62.

22 *VCH: Hertfordshire*, 314.

23 HALSC, D/End F50.

24 HALSC, D/ECd F60.

25 Roscoe, 'James "Athenian" Stuart', 184.

26 A joint monument at St Mary, Aspenden, commemorates the first Fremans to own land in the area, the brothers Ralph (d.1634) and William (d.1623). N. Pevsner and B. Cherry, *The Buildings of England: Hertfordshire* (Harmondsworth, 1978), 77–78.

27 *VCH: Hertfordshire*, 315; Smith, *Braughing*, 16.

28 The most accurate source is the family tree that Charles Cocks had drawn up when he was raised to the peerage as Baron Somers in 1784. Eastnor Castle, Cocks Manuscripts, Genealogical Table – Somers-Cocks, shelfmark 18.6.18. I am grateful to Mr James Hervey-Bathurst for granting me access and to the archivist Hazel Lein for her help with the Cocks papers at Eastnor Castle.

29 C. J. Robinson, *A History of the Mansions and Manors of Herefordshire* (Little Logaston, Logaston, Woonton, Almeley, 2001), 119.

30 Charles Cocks was MP for Reigate 1747–84, Philip Yorke from 1741–47 when he was replaced by Charles Yorke 1747–68 and then John Yorke 1768–84. Between them, the Yorkes and Cockses owned almost all the burgage tenements in Reigate and all elections after 1722 were uncontested, with each family nominating one MP apiece. See Surrey History Centre, Catalogue of the Cocks papers, 371, Somers Cocks Family of Reigate Priory: Estate Records, Including Manors of Reigate and Reigate Priory, and Burgage Tenements in Reigate, 1400–1911, and Papers of John Somers (1651–1716), First Baron Somers, Lord Chancellor, 1676–c.1745; Sedgwick, *House of Commons*, 2, 562–63; Namier and Brooke, *House of Commons*, 3, 387.

31 BL, Add. MS 35,610, fols.7–8, Charles Cocks to Philip Yorke, second earl of Hardwicke, undated.

32 N. Pevsner, *The Buildings of England: Herefordshire* (Harmondsworth, 1963), 122.

33 Eastnor Castle, Cocks Manuscripts, Cocks Box 1: Charles Cocks 1st Baron, Charles Yorke to Charles Cocks, 8 August 1766.

34 BL, Add. MS 35,638, fol.17, Charles Cocks to Charles Yorke, 19 August 1766.

35 Eastnor Castle, Cocks Manuscripts, Cocks Box 1: Charles Cocks 1st Baron, Charles Yorke to [Charles Cocks], 7 October 1766.

36 BL, Add. MS 35,638, fol.37, Charles Cocks to Charles Yorke, 8 November 1766, in which is transcribed a letter from Joseph Cocks to his brother. See also BL, Add. MS 35,638, fol.58, Charles Cocks to Charles Yorke, 25 January 1767.

37 The other trustees were John Somers Cocks (son and heir of Charles Cocks) and Revd Philip Cocks. Eastnor Castle, Cocks Manuscripts, Stray Deeds Box 1, Declaration of Trust from Miss Eliza Cocks, The Honble John Somers Cocks & the Rev Philip Cocks July 29 1789.

# Mourning the dead in the nineteenth century: Neoclassical, Romantic and Gothic Revival monuments

*Jane Kelsall*

*They are the silent griefs which cut the heart-strings*
*(J. Ford,* The Broken Heart, *Act V, Sc 3)*[1]

*Jane Kelsall is a lecturer in Art History, guide at St Albans Cathedral and guide book author.*

GRAND AND OPERATIC STYLES of memorial sculpture faded from fashion in the last half of the eighteenth century. The scholar Winckelmann having reappraised much of the Vatican collection thought that many sculptures there were Roman copies of lost Greek originals. Archaeological discoveries of ancient Greek statues endorsed Winckelmann's findings. The English milords on their Grand Tours were converted and abandoned the grandeur of Rome for the glory of Greece. Florid monuments of coloured imported marble, usually showing men in public life gesturing as if taking part in an opera in stone, were made no more for British churches (Fig. 1). The Latin inscriptions, incomprehensible to most, trumpeting the grand pedigrees and noble deeds of the deceased, were abandoned for English texts in a different mood with a different message.

White marble was the chosen material for the new Neoclassical style monuments, sometimes with a plain black border. Some were still made to commemorate the great and the good, such as the heroes of the Napoleonic wars. These were now presented in classical mode; they sometimes teeter on the edge of solemnity – and then collapse into the ridiculous. Thomas Banks' memorial in St Paul's cathedral to Captain Westcott (d.1805) is a good example. A scene from The Battle of the Nile is depicted in bas-relief on the plinth, excellently carved. Unfortunately the free-standing life-sized figure of Westcott, half-naked in a short chiton (instead of his dignified naval uniform) is shown dying in the arms of Victory, who seems unable to support him (Fig. 2). Instead of invoking feelings of sadness for the loss of a brave hero, spectators reacted by laughing at such creations and our later war memorials changed to sombre tableaux, usually of soldiers with bowed heads guarding a coffin.

From early medieval times some monuments had been ordered, paid for and installed during the lifetime of the departed. This ensured that the memorial was just what a patron wanted and that money set aside for a monument was not appropriated by the heirs. This practice of ordering one's own tomb gradually fell out of favour and was greatly disapproved of by the 1770s.[2] Instead, monuments were ordered from a sculptor's studio by surviving members of the family, so a new emphasis on mourning

*Fig. 1: The Duke of Chandos and his two wives (1718) by Grinling Gibbons, at St Lawrence, Little Stanmore, Middlesex.*

is understandable. Instead of a life-size portrait statue of the deceased, smaller wall-hung monuments gained in popularity, some with a medallion bas-relief portrait of the deceased and others with the figure of the deceased held by a classically draped female. Often the supporting figure weeps over a broken column, the symbol of a life cut short. Sometimes she is the muse of history or literature if that seemed appropriate to the interests of the deceased. She has no wings, as representations of angels were deemed imprudent in Protestant England, although a few had begun to creep back on church monuments from the seventeenth century onwards. The origin of the mourning lady was taken by sculptors, like cherubs, 'from the Antique', thus deflecting accusations of popery. The mourning lady may also represent the Virtue of the deceased: Addison wrote that 'your virtues are generally shown in petticoats'.[3] The texts on Neoclassical monuments now express quiet regret for the dear departed with less prominent heraldry. Another popular feature was an imitation of the Greek *stele*, outdoor monuments found in Greece, with a rectangular outline topped with a shallow pediment, often with anthemion motifs and acanthus leaves. And there are many moving memorials to women who died in childbirth and to little children.[4] Why?

*Fig. 2: Captain Westcott (1802–5) by Thomas Banks, at St Paul's Cathedral, London.*

The French Revolution had sent shock-waves through the British upper classes. Many blamed the blatantly licentious behaviour of the idle French aristocracy for their downfall. It was time for the British ruling class to set a good example to possible revolutionaries and live a decent private life. Queen Victoria's wicked uncles, a rich source of material for cartoonists and satirists, were replaced by Victoria and Albert's clear example of hard work and domestic virtue. The increased mobility of the upper classes from the late eighteenth century onwards had allowed more love-matches in marriage, so the death of a beloved wife or husband was hard to bear. Monuments were needed as a focus for grief. A little child's death was mourned in a more public way. *Sensibility* came into fashion, promoted by Rousseau's belief in the truth of natural feeling and emotion. Novels by Richardson (*Pamela* 1740 and *Clarissa* 1748) were best-sellers. The novel, a

*Fig. 3: Penelope Boothby (1793) by Thomas Banks, at St Oswald, Ashbourne, Derbyshire.*

new art form, showed people a different way to feel and behave. Banks' famous monument to five-year-old Penelope Boothby (d.1791) (Fig. 3) is an example. This masterpiece influenced sculptors and patrons alike.[5] Here we have an effigy on a tomb chest, a rarity in monuments since the Reformation; but, as in the parable of the Raising of Jairus' daughter, 'she is not dead, but sleepeth'. Penelope lies on her side in a naturalistic way, wearing a muslin dress with a wide sash. Her arms are bent with the hands near her face, the fingers softly curled. Although the white marble is polished and cold, Banks has inhabited his sculpture with astonishing pathos. Surely she will soon awaken? No wonder Queen Charlotte and her daughters wept when the tomb was exhibited at the Royal Academy in London before it was installed at Ashbourne, Derbyshire. This Neoclassical memorial marks the appearance of the Romantic Naturalism which makes many nineteenth-century monuments memorable. Penelope's father, Sir Brooke Boothby, pretentiously had the text engraved on the tomb chest of his daughter in Italian. It was written by Edmund Burke, Boothby's political rival but clearly an admirer of the little girl. The translation provided tells us that 'She was in form and intellect most exquisite. The unfortunate parents ventured their all upon this frail barque and the wreck was total'. And indeed

*Fig. 4: Wall monuments in the north transept of Brecon Cathedral.*

Sir Brooke Boothby and his wife Susanna, who were united only in the love of their only child, parted at the graveside never to meet again.

Looking at the north transept of Brecon cathedral there is an interesting display of wall monuments revealing many features of early nineteenth-century sculpture (Fig. 4). Three are in Neoclassical style, showing urns – symbolic of the grave, a popular 'antique' feature since the mid seventeenth century. On the right is the monument to Susanna Watkins (d.1847). A mourning female figure weeps beside an urn, while the sunburst behind speaks of glory in Heaven, where the loved one now resides. These ubiquitous ladies and urns are usually dull. The upper central monument showing Mr George Price Watkins contemplating two urns representing his parents do not move the spectator but perhaps comforted the donor. Yet the urn above the bas-relief tableau on the monument (first from right) to the Revd Thomas Watkins (d.1829) by J. E. Thomas, although not of the best quality, nevertheless shows an interesting scene as this father on his deathbed is awaited in Heaven by his son and daughter, winged in angelic form.

The central lower monument in the Brecon group shows a woman and two children locked in sorrow at the deathbed of their benefactor, George Price Watkins (d.1843), who had been a generous donor to the poor. It is like a page from an illustrated novel – a key scene with text and sculpture involving the spectator in the story of personal grief. As the Victorians devoured more novels, such visual narratives become more frequent in church memorials.

To the left is a tableau of a young married woman, Sophia Watkins (d.1851) by J. E. Thomas. Sophia is being escorted to Heaven by an angel – an astonishing visual reference to the Assumption of the Virgin, a favourite Roman Catholic subject in art which is without biblical substance. This design became very popular for a young girl's memorial and was used by several sculptors.[6] It seems that angels were settling back on to monuments, apparently with acceptable Catholic symbolism. Angels direct only women to Heaven on Victorian monuments; perhaps men know the way.

This return of angels as a commonplace in the nineteenth century was promoted by John Flaxman (1755–1826), the first English sculptor to gain an international reputation. He worked for Josiah Wedgwood on the classical friezes of figures on his jasperware. Studying in Rome, Flaxman was much affected by sculptural angels in the churches, especially those of Canova (1757–1822) on the Stuart monument (1819) in St Peter's. On his return he incorporated angels into his church memorials. Flaxman's angels were popular and as a devout Protestant with Swedenborgian leanings, no one could accuse him of popery. Baroque and Rococo monuments had mostly avoided any religious imagery or texts, and indeed, most seventeenth-century monuments would not look out of place in a town hall. By the nineteenth century greater religious tolerance had overcome post-Reformation anxieties and those who ordered monuments, like the Watkins family at Brecon, could ask monumental sculptors to refer to Christianity once more. An angel is a timeless symbol of Christian comfort to people and indeed was used as a symbolic refuge from industrial life. In the late nineteenth century Burne-Jones remarked that every time he saw telegraph poles going up he went home and drew more angels.

At Christchurch Priory, Hampshire, Henry Weekes' free-standing memorial (1854) to Percy Bysshe Shelley shows life-size figures of the muse of poetry cradling the poet's body (Fig. 5). Her face is remarkably like his wife Mary, who was not with him when he drowned in the Gulf of Spezia in 1822. Yet this conceit of Romantic Naturalism is acceptable, although what the atheist poet would have thought of his memorial in a church we cannot know. No doubt he would have been amused that it had been turned away by the local clergy from Bournemouth St Peter, near his parents' home, the church for which it was intended. The pose

*Fig. 5: Percy Bysshe Shelley (1854) by Weekes, at Christchurch Priory, Hampshire.*

depicting Shelley as Christ and his wife as the Virgin in a *pieta* was not countenanced. However Mary's exemplary widowhood and persistent sanitising of her husband's biography persuaded nearby Christchurch to admit it to the base of their tower, although not to the main body of the church. People wanted to believe that Shelley was 'good' when they saw Weekes' beautiful Romantic sculpture. And had he not written

> *Heaven's light forever shines, earth's shadows fly;*
> *Life, like a many-coloured glass,*
> *Stains the white radiance of eternity.*[7]

His later effigial memorial in University College chapel, Oxford, by Onslow Ford in 1894 was made sufficiently long after he had been ejected as an atheist from the university for that transgression to be forgotten, apparently. It was originally intended for the Protestant cemetery in Rome.

Matthew Boulton (who admired Keats' poetry) and his family must have been greatly comforted by the monument to his wife Mary Ann (d.1829 age 43) by Sir Francis Chantry (1834) at Great Tew, Oxfordshire (Fig. 6). Enhanced by a perfect woodland setting, the opening of the door of the church reveals the lady reclining on a Grecian couch, meditating on a book that she is reading. On a fine day she is radiant in the sunlight.

> *She cannot fade, though thou hast not thy bliss,*
> *For ever wilt thou love and she be fair.*[8]

This monument has Gothic decorations on the tomb chest and in the niche. The Gothic Revival was passionately promoted by A. W. G. Pugin (1812–52) who disliked Baroque and Classical

*Fig. 6: Mary Ann Boulton (1829) by Sir Francis Chantry, at St Michael & All Angels, Great Tew, Oxfordshire.*

architecture and monuments because of their continental origin. Britain's superior native style was Gothic, he proclaimed, and churches must be returned to their medieval layout, with all significant features. The lonely voice of the architect George Whittington correctly cited the Gothic style as originating in twelfth-century France, but the Gothic Revival bandwagon was rolling, aided by the Oxford Movement and the Cambridge Camden Society, and no one wanted an unpalatable truth to get in the way of a popular national revival movement.

Many of the ruling classes were enthusiastically involved in promoting changes to church services and to church restoration which was a new concept: the word *restoration* – with reference to a building – does not enter the language until about this time. It was important to engage an educated architect – a new breed – to ensure that correct Gothic features were rebuilt. Some built new churches in the Cambridge Camden Society approved style. Many wanted medieval monuments for themselves with an effigy, tomb chest and a canopy. Before the Reformation, effigies with hands together had been a visual reminder to the community to constantly celebrate masses for the soul of the departed. Yet the doctrine of Purgatory was alien to the Church of England so it seemed inappropriate for most people to show a prone praying effigy on nineteenth-century monuments.

John Cust, first Earl Brownlow (1779–1853), was described by J. P. Neale as 'an accomplished and polite scholar'. He wished to continue his family's tradition of monuments at Belton, Lincolnshire and commissioned the great Antonio Canova to make an enormous marble Neoclassical statue of 'Christian Religion' to commemorate his first wife, the heiress Sophia Hume (d.1814), the mother of his two sons and a daughter (Fig. 7). This

*Fig. 7.  Sophia Lady Brownlow (1814) by Antonio Canova, at St Peter & St Paul, Belton, Lincolnshire*

*Fig. 8: Caroline Lady Brownlow (1824) by Sir Richard Westmacott, at St Peter & St Paul, Belton, Lincolnshire.*

impressive figure points with her right hand to Heaven (originally she held a cross and wore a pointed diadem, which have not survived) while her left hand rests on a column bearing a medallion portrait of Sophia. It is one of only two monuments by Canova in English churches. When John Cust's second wife Caroline died in 1824 he commissioned Sir Richard Westmacott, a pupil of Canova (who had died in 1822) to make a modest wall monument (she produced only three daughters) in bas-relief, showing a Romantic and much more personal portrait figure of Caroline with a pilgrim's hat and staff, with four cherubs above her head (Fig. 8). When considering his own tomb, John Cust commissioned Baron Carlo Marochetti, who had followed King Louis Philippe from France into exile in England in 1848. Marochetti had impressed the English with his life-size Gothic Revival statue of Richard the Lionheart for the Great Exhibition. Richard, brandishing a sword, is seated on a fine horse. This statue was later copied in bronze and stands outside the Palace of Westminster.

The monument to John Cust, first Earl Brownlow, is Gothic Revival in all its colourful grandeur (Fig. 9). The superbly carved white marble effigy lies prone with hands together in prayer. He wears the robes and coronet of an earl and lies on a tomb chest of pink marble with metal heraldic plaques. It is one of many such monuments of 1850–1920, showing portrait effigies, sometimes of a married couple, firmly placing themselves in the medieval tradition but with Victorian additions such as family pets at the feet instead of heraldic animals. They also look their age when they died, except the fifty-six-year-old Corisande, countess of Malmesbury, at Christchurch, Hampshire. The face on her

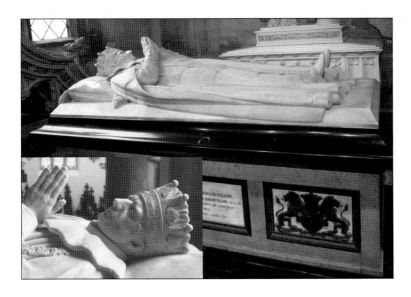

*Fig. 9: John Cust, first Earl Brownlow (1853) by Baron Carlo Marochetti, at St Peter & St Paul, Belton, Lincolnshire.*

*Fig. 10: Corisande, Countess of Malmesbury (1876) by Gaetano Trentanove, at Christchurch, Hampshire.*

sleeping effigy, finely carved by Gaetano Trentanove in 1876, is that of a woman aged thirty three (the perfect age of Christ) (Fig. 10); she approved of *that* medieval tradition. Most of the effigies lie as if sleeping with their heads on one side with relaxed hands, which perhaps involves the mourners more personally than the more rigid prayer position. Many Victorian effigies of churchmen in cathedrals lie with one hand on the breast with the other by the side, sometimes holding a book. Interestingly, not one of the bishops, deans or archdeacons has his wife beside him, perhaps in imitation of monuments of the celibate medieval clergy. Often there is a strange mixture of styles, where antique, medieval Gothic and Gothic Revival are put together. For example, Archdeacon Henry Moore's effigy (1876) at Lichfield cathedral, Staffordshire lies peacefully in a decorated style niche on a tomb chest (Fig. 11) very like that of Pope Clement IV (*c.*1271–4) at St Peter's, Rome, with roundels of porphyry and pre-Cosmati work. It was designed by Sir G. G. Scott and carved by Armstead who has kindly made Henry look a little younger than his eighty years.

There is no place for sentiment on Gothic Revival monuments of sedate churchmen and aristocrats, but it survives occasionally, for example on the monument at Tickhill, Yorkshire, to Louisa Blanche Foljambe (d.1871 age 29). Louisa married Cecil Foljambe in 1869 and their son Arthur was born in 1870. A second son, Frederick, was born in 1871 but lived for only one day. Six weeks later Louisa herself died and her husband commissioned William Calder Marshall to make her tomb with an effigy on a Gothic Revival tomb chest. It cannot have been an easy task for Calder Marshall, as his own wife had died in the same

*Fig. 11: Archdeacon Henry Moore (1876) by Henry Armstead, designed by Sir George Gilbert Scott, at Lichfield cathedral, Staffordshire.*

circumstances. Louisa's recumbent robed figure lies cradling Frederick in her arm (Fig. 12). It has been carved from pink veined alabaster which lies on a tomb chest decorated with ogee arches supported by columns with heraldic shields between them. Religious texts are engraved on the table top and words from a hymn of Horatius Bonar on the plinth. The monument was placed in the north-east chapel at Haselbech, Northamptonshire where other members of the Foljambe family lie. Years later, when the family sold the remote Haselbech estate, her son Arthur, second earl of Liverpool, wanted to move the monument to Tickhill. Sympathetic Foljambes were patrons of the church at Tickhill. Hence, in 1908, it was moved at great expense, after faculties had been obtained.

Over the next 28 years after Louisa's death Cecil Foljambe also commissioned no less that 62 inscribed brass plates and heraldic shields in stone and glass in 38 churches in England to commemorate his 'beloved wife'.[9] It is hard to say which is the more extraordinary: the 62 memorials or the moving of the tomb. Clearly Cecil was distraught at his wife's death although he married again six years later and his second wife Susan, Louisa's cousin, produced eleven children. Clearly Arthur never forgot his mother, but why move the tomb? Was it solely the sale of the Haselbech estate? We can only surmise that he could not bear his mother to be left among strangers. Although he never lived at Tickhill – his career in the army and as Governor-General in New Zealand kept him on the move – he must have wanted Louisa and Frederick to be seen and admired, which indeed they are.[10]

*Fig. 12: Louisa Blanche Foljambe and Frederick (1871) by William Calder Marshall, at St Mary, Tickhill, Yorkshire. Photo: C B Newham*

Another visual reminder of long-lasting grief can be seen at Essendon, Hertfordshire, where two little effigies of sleeping babies lie (Fig. 13). They are Robert and Laura Hanbury who died in 1866 and 1868. There were no other children. It was not until 1888 that their parents commissioned William Theed, a renowned and expensive sculptor, to make the likenesses. Perhaps it finally brought comfort to the parents.[11] Their mother Frances became patron of the local orphanage.

*Fig. 13: Robert and Laura Hanbury (d. 1866 and 1868) by William Theed, at St Mary, Essendon, Hertfordshire.*

At the end of the nineteenth century mourning families felt a growing need for useful memorials. At Childwickbury, Hertfordshire, a tiny estate church near St Albans, the font commemorates Winifred and Dorothy Blundell Maple age eight and six. Winifred died of scarlet fever in 1886 and Dorothy of diphtheria in 1888. Fortunately another daughter survived. The alabaster sculpture (Fig. 14) shows Winifred kneeling, holding a large shell, big enough for a font bowl, while her sister stands behind with a hand on Winifred's shoulder. Both have been given wings.[12] Their parents then built the Sisters Hospital in St Albans.

This trend for useful memorials continued and there are few twentieth-century sculptural monuments. Now churches usually

Fig. 14: Winifred and Dorothy Blundell Maple (d. 1886 and 1888), at St Mary, Childwickbury, Hertfordshire.

spend legacies on repairing the central heating or mending a leaking roof. Occasionally a communion chalice is bought and engraved 'In loving memory…' but that is all, even for Princess Diana.

## Acknowledgements

*I am grateful to my husband, David Kelsall, for photography (except Figure 12).*

## Notes

1  J. Ford, *The Broken Heart* in Regents Renaissance Drama Series (ed. Donald Anderson), (1968), Act V, Sc 3, 74.

2  The parishioners of St Stephen Walbrook, London, insisted at this date that J. F. Moore's monument to Mrs Macauley was taken down as soon as it was erected, as she was still alive.

3  J. Addison, *Dialogue upon the Usefulness of Ancient Medals in Works* (1811), 360.

4  For death in childbirth, e.g. to Mrs Morley (1784) by John Flaxman at Gloucester Cathedral; Frances Princess Bariatinsky (d.1807) by John Bacon Jnr at St Mary Magdalene, Sherborne, Gloucestershire; Anna Maria Rooke Greaves (d.1819) by Sir Francis Chantry at St Mary, Waterperry, Oxfordshire; Georgiana Caldecott (d.1846) by E. H. Baily at St Mary, Baldock, Hertfordshire. There are others.

5  cf 'The Sleeping Children' (1817) by Chantry at Lichfield Cathedral, Staffordshire.

6  Some designs were repeated all over Britain for different clients and were cheaper than an individual memorial.

7  P. B. Shelley, *Adonais*, in *Selections of English Romantic Poets* (Cambridge, 1920), 71.

8  J. Keats, *Ode on a Grecian Urn*, in *The Poetical Works of J. Keats* (OUP, 1973), 223.

9  Her remains, and those of little Frederick, stayed buried at another family church at Scrofton, Nottinghamshire where they were interred in the family vault in 1871.

10  Revd D. Thorpe, *The Beloved Wife* (Tickhill and District Local History Society, 2007).

11  The faculty for Theed's sculpture is dated 1919 which may indicate that it was not procured until after the Great War. The mother died in 1916, when the sculpture may have been given to the church.

12  The sculpture is unsigned and there is no faculty or newspaper report of its installation.

# Pastiche or fake? A sub-Gill monument at Brandwood End Cemetery, Birmingham

*Julian W. S. Litten*

*Julian Litten is a Vice-President of the Church Monuments Society.*

A MONUMENT ERECTED at Brandwood End Cemetery, Birmingham in 1939 bears an almost too-coincidental likeness to one of 1934 by Eric Gill at Cranham, Gloucestershire. Is the monument at Birmingham also by Gill, or could it be a faithful copy by another sculptor?

On 14 February 1934, Dixon Henry Davies of Cranham, Gloucestershire died. Following his funeral service at St James, Cranham he was buried in the south-west corner of the churchyard and, subsequently, a raised ledger in Portland stone, to the design of Eric Gill (1882–1940), was erected above his grave (Fig. 1).

Dixon Henry Davies does not appear in the *Dictionary of National Biography*, but we do know that he was born on 3 January 1859, one of four sons of John Whitridge Davies and Susan Gregory of Oswestry, Shropshire. Two of his other brothers were Edward Harold Davies (d.1947), Professor of Music at the University of Adelaide, Australia and the composer Sir Henry Walford Davies (1869–1941). One assumes, therefore, that as Edward Davies was probably residing in Adelaide at the time of his brother's death, that it was Henry Walford Davies who was responsible for commissioning the monument, though it is not recorded whether or not he personally knew Eric Gill. At the time of Dixon Davies' death, Gill was working from his new studio at Piggots, near High Wycombe, Buckinghamshire, having moved there in 1928 from Spoil Bank, Ditchling, Sussex.

The village of Cranham holds a minor place in the history of the Arts & Crafts movement. The composer Gustav Holst (1874–1934) lived there for a while, and it was there, in the house now called Midwinter Cottage, that he wrote his famous tune 'Cranham' to Christina Rossetti's poem *In the bleak midwinter*. In addition, the poet and composer Ivor Gurney (1890–1937) came from nearby Gloucester, whilst Sapperton, a few miles to the south east and the nub of the Cotswold Arts & Crafts movement, was where Ernest Gimson (1864–1919) and the brothers Ernest (1863–1926) and Sidney Barnsley (1865–1926) had their studios. Chipping Campden, some fifteen miles to the north-east, was where C. R. Ashbee (1863–1942) had his Guild of Handicraft 1902–1907.

Regardless of these artistic associations, it may well be that the reason for selecting Gill lay not so much with personal contact than the existence of an artists' collective known as 'Sculpture and

*Fig. 1: The Davies monument by Eric Gill at Cranham, Gloucestershire. Above, as seen from the east; below, from the west. Photos: Sally Badham*

Memorials'.[1] The preface by the Very Revd Foxley Norris, Dean of Westminster, to the 1938 third edition of their illustrated catalogue, explains their beginnings and their aims:[2]

> Inaugurated by a small group of artists in 1934 on a very modest scale our effort was to recapture something of the artistic feeling and fine taste which made our churchyards beautiful 200 years ago. The venture has so far succeeded. It has not only been shown to meet a very definite want, but has developed in ways we had not contemplated. The move to more commodious and convenient quarters in Albermarle Street marks an epoch in our career and will we hope, give us the opportunity for providing that which for long has been a crying need – a place where contemporary sculpture can be seen and its adaptability to many purposes appreciated. Of all forms of art Sculpture has been the least fortunate in this respect. Painters and musicians are well provided with opportunities for displaying their achievements. Sculptors have almost none outside their own studios.
>
> Meanwhile good lettering – and there are few things more important – and simple artistic treatment of homely materials are becoming more and more widely appreciated and generally desired: and if our effort does something to meet these desires and to encourage local craftsmen we shall not have lived in vain.

This enterprising venture, the forerunner of Harriet Fraser's Memorials by Artists, had the approbation of the Central Council for the Care of Churches, their letter of recommendation being published in the first edition of the Sculpture and Memorials catalogue:[3]

> This organisation, which is a serious attempt to create a widespread movement towards the revival of the craft of the mason and sculptor, has been considered by the Central Council for the Care of Churches. In their opinion a scheme such as this is clearly worthy of support and encouragement, and should do much to help the efforts of the Diocesan Advisory Committees, and of others who are working for the improvement of our churches and churchyards. We have every hope that by its example it will encourage the use of local material and will help to improve the standard of churchyard memorials.

E. F. Hitchcock was appointed to direct the business side of the venture, with the sculptor Gilbert Ledward directing the technical side of the organisation. The foundation advisory committee consisted of:

The Very Revd W Foxley Norris, CVO, DD, Dean of Westminster and Chairman of the Central Council for the Care of Churches

Mr (later Sir) E. Guy Dawber ARA, PPRIBA, Chairman of the Council for the Preservation of Rural England

Mr (later Sir) Gilbert Ledward, ARA, FRBS

Sir Edwin Lutyens, KCIE, RA, DCL, LLD

Mr Evelyn Shaw, CVVO, LLD, Hon Secretary of The British School at Rome

By 1938 both Foxley Norris and Guy Dawber were dead, their places having being taken Eric Gill, ARA, RDI, HonARIBA, ARBS and Professor (later Sir) Albert E. Richardson, ARA, FRIBA.

The list of artists providing designs and sculpture for Sculpture and Memorials is formidable. The 1934 illustrated catalogue showed examples by Julian P. Allan, A. J. Ayres, E. Guy Dawber, Richard Garbe, Eric Gill, Allan Howes, Gilbert Ledward, H. Parr and Newbury A. Trent. By 1938 this had been extended to include Joseph Cribb, Reginald E. Dark, Alan Durst, George Friend, Macdonald Gill, Bennett Ingram, C. D.'O. Pilkington Jackson, David Kindersley, Herbert Palliser, Donald Potter, Hilary Stratton, Edmund Ware and Ernest Webb.

Of importance to this paper are three sketches for substantial churchyard tombs by Eric Gill, dated November 1932, and illustrated on page 52 of the 1938 catalogue. One of these (Fig. 2) shows a design which was to be subsequently selected for the tomb in Cranham churchyard for the grave of Dixon Henry Davies (d.1934). It is of a stone ledger, chamfered on the underside, and raised from the ground by blocks of stone at its east and west ends. In form, it is a variant of the table-tomb. Inscribed on the eastern edge of the ledger are the words 'REQUIESCAT IN PACE', and along the northern edge 'I BELIEVE IN THE HOLY GHOST; LORD AND GIVER OF LIFE'. Could it be that these three designs were created by Gill for Walford Davies to select from during the preliminary negotiations for the Cranham monument?

Comparing this sketch with the finished tomb, two slight alterations took place between the date of the 1932 sketch and the monument coming off the chisel in 1934, as can be seen in the photograph of the monument on page 51 of the 1938 catalogue (Fig. 3). The first is that Gill made the central cross on the upper surface of the raised ledger to be in relief rather than incised; an expensive modification, as this would have entailed cutting away almost the entire surface of the stone to achieve the required effect. Second, the supportive legs were tapered on their north and south elevations. The west edge of the ledger is inscribed 'DIXON HENRY DAVIES', and the north side. 'BORN JANUARY 3 1859 – DIED FEBRUARY 14 1934' followed by three Gill olive leaves, now mostly obscured by lichen.

The monument above Plot 228 in Section B6 CE at Brandwood End Cemetery, Woodthorpe Road, King's Heath,

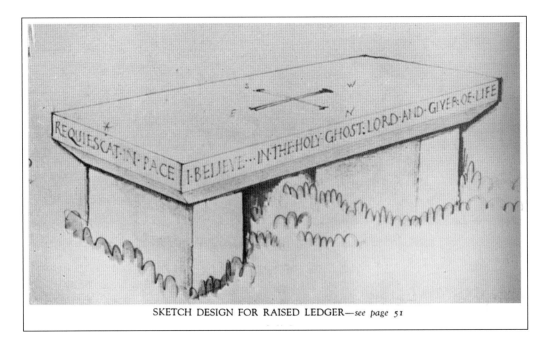

SKETCH DESIGN FOR RAISED LEDGER—*see page 51*

Eric Gill, A.R.A., R.D.I.                                    Portland Stone

A SIMPLE BUT EFFECTIVE DESIGN—*see sketch on page 52*

*Fig. 2 (top): Eric Gill's 1932 sketch design for a raised ledger.*
*Fig. 3 (bottom): the Davies monument as executed. Both from* Sculptured Memorials and Headstones *(3rd edn., 1938), 51, 52.*

Birmingham to the three Atkins sisters (Fig. 4) is identical in every respect to that of Dixon Henry Davies at Cranham. Its faithfulness to the original Gill sketch of 1932 is borne out by the inscription – 'REQUIESCAT IN PACE' – along the western edge of the raised ledger. The whole, including the crazy-paving landing stone, is made not of Portland stone but of brown Hornton stone, and sits on top of a lower slab of York stone, capping an earth grave. Hornton stone was an excellent choice, as it is native to Warwickshire and is particularly responsive to deep carving and lettering.

The inscription along the north edge of the raised ledger reads:

BORN MAY 4TH 1882   ANNIE EDITH ATKINS   DIED JUNE 27TH 1938

and that along the south:

BORN MARCH 2ND 1886   ALICE GERTRUDE ATKINS

DIED NOV 13TH 1938

A further inscription, on the south side of the upper surface of the raised ledger, reads:

BORN JAN 11TH 1888   WINIFRED MARY LANDUCCI

DIED SEPT 16TH 1964

and again on the upper surface of the raised ledger, at its east end:

IN MEMORY OF
F H LANDUCCI
1/5 ROYAL WARWICKSHIRE REGT
KILLED IN ACTION
AT THE SOMME
JULY 16TH 1916

*Fig. 4: The Atkins monument at Brandwood End Cemetery, Birmingham. Photo: Julian Litten*

147

The lettering along the edges of the ledger stone are finely cut, but those on the top surface lack the same confidence, dictating two chisels at work. Furthermore, a close examination of the monument shows that there is a feint signature at the north end of the bottom of the west face of the supporting west slab: 'H L MARKS' (Fig. 5).

H. L. Marks's monumental masonry works have been by the entrance gates to Brandwood End Cemetery since the 1890s. According to Steve Bamford, the present managing director, the company's records were destroyed by fire in the 1970s, thus the client file relating to the Atkins monument no longer survives. However, from an examination of the lettering,[4] Mr Bamford was of the opinion that the inscription might have been cut by Leonard Marks, the son of Harry L. Marks, the founder of the firm, who had studied letter-cutting under the Birmingham sculptor, William H. Bloye (1890–1975). However, none of the other monuments at Brandwood End supplied by H. L. Marks has

*Fig. 5: The feint signature of H L Marks on the Atkins monument at Brandwood End, Birmingham. Photo: Julian Litten*

letter-cutting of comparative elegance, and on balance it would appear that H. L. Marks merely banked the ledger and contracted out the letter-cutting to William H. Bloye, who would have been forty-nine years of age in 1939 when the monument was commissioned. Bloye, who had studied at Birmingham School of Art before the Great War, also spent time studying with Eric Gill in *c.*1921, whose influence can be detected in Bloye's reliefs of 1925 in Birmingham's Hall of Memory.[5]

The loss of the client's file at Messrs Marks forces us to speculate how the Atkins monument came into being. One can presume that, requiring a high-quality contemporary monument for her two recently deceased sisters, the widowed Mrs Landucci (nèe Atkins) was shown or lent a copy of the 1938 third edition Sculpture and Memorials catalogue in H. L. Marks's possession, as the Gill monument to Davies does not appear in either the August 1934 first edition nor in the October 1937 second edition.[6] This helps to date the commission to post September 1938, corroborated by the cemetery ledgers recording the issue of a permit for the erection of a monument on Plot 228 Section B6.CE on 6 June 1939, thereby allowing for the statutory six months for the grave to settle. One has to be grateful that H. L. Marks placed their signature to the tomb for had they not then there is every possibility that the Atkins monument might have ended up as being a discovery of a previously unrecorded piece by Eric Gill. Were that the case then it would almost certainly have been his last example of letter-cutting prior to his death in 1940. Yet what is more astounding is the audacity of H. L Marks in lifting a copyright design from under the nose of a living sculptor. In their defence, England's economy was at that time in straitened circumstances, the Sculpture Centre itself was on the brink of closure and H. L. Marks could hardly be expected to give up a rare and lucrative commission at a time of national stringency. Consequently, the niceties of copyright were bypassed. It was probably as a safeguard from possible prosecution that they added their signature to the finished work.

That Winifred Landucci also intended to be buried in her sisters' grave explains its designation in the cemetery records as purchase for four 'full burial' spaces.[7] It is to be regretted that by the time of Winifred Landucci's death in 1964 William Bloye had retired, as her inscription,[8] and that to her husband who had been killed on the Somme in 1916,[9] departs from the elegance of Bloye's chisel. As for the tomb's status, it is a pastiche; had it not been signed by H. L. Marks then it would rightly have been designated the soubriquet of a 'fake'.

**Notes**

1 Established in 1934 and trading as 'Sculptured Memorials and Headstones' from 12 Lower Regent Street, London SW1. In 1937 they moved to The Sculpture Centre, 26 Albermarle Street, London W1 where they traded as 'Sculpture and Memorials'. It appears that the venture closed shortly after the outbreak of World War II in 1939.

2 *Sculptured Memorials and Headstones* (3rd edition, 1938).

3 *Sculptured Memorials and Headstones* (1st edition, 1934).

4 In the presence of the author on 25 August 2009.

5 G. Archer, *The Glorious Dead: Figurative Sculpture of British First World War Memorials* (Kirkstead, 2009), 120-21, pl.106.

6 *Sculptured Memorials and Headstones* (2nd edition, 1937).

7 The clerk at Brandwood End Cemetery informs me that 'full burial' interprets as corporeal burial, which is to say burial of a body in a coffin rather than that of cremated remains.

8 The permit for the additional inscription to Winifred M. Landucci was issued on 16 October 1964.

9 The permit for the additional inscription to F. H. Landucci was issued on 6 July 1965.

# Book reviews

Alan Brookes and Nikolaus Pevsner, *The Buildings of England: Worcestershire*. Yale, 2007, 846 pp., 132 col. plates, £29.95 hdbk, ISBN 978 0 300 11298 6; John Gifford, *The Buildings of Scotland: Perth and Kinross*. Yale, 2007, 802 pp., 126 col. plates, £29.95 hdbk, ISBN 978 0 300 10922 1.

The two volumes under review were published within a few weeks of each other, and reviewing them together provides an opportunity to reflect on similarities and differences in the treatment of ecclesiastical architecture in the English and Scottish series of the enterprise begun over half a century ago by Sir Nikolaus Pevsner. *Worcestershire* is the second, enlarged edition, of a volume first produced in 1968, while *Perth and Kinross* is the pioneer for its area. Both volumes are produced to the high standard we have come to expect of the series.

One of the great achievements of the Scottish series is that, without pandering to a Nationalist agenda, it has brought the built heritage of Scotland in from the cold, and has made easily accessible an unsuspected quantity of architecturally and historically significant buildings. When the first volume was published, thirty years ago, it was intended that the country should be covered in ten volumes; *Perth and Kinross* is the tenth, but the task is only about two-thirds achieved. As in England, much of the expansion has been caused by depth of research greater than originally envisaged, and by a widening appreciation of what is significant, particularly in relation to the nineteenth century. Comparison between the two editions of Worcestershire is instructive in this respect: while the older book refers to the work of Butterfield at St Lawrence in the ancient village of Alvechurch, the newer one sets it in its context, enthuses about it, and believes it to be amongst the architect's best work; the neighbouring nineteenth-century outer suburb of Birmingham, Barnt Green, is dismissed in 11 lines of the old book, the basilican St Andrew's of 1909–14 simply noted, while the new one gives 16 lines and a diagram to the church and four pages to the settlement as a whole.

Despite the discovery of so much in Scotland, the density of the built heritage is significantly lower than in most of England. Worcestershire is one of the smaller English counties, at 738 square miles (the area covered by the 2007 book is smaller as part of the north east has been hived off to appear in *Birmingham and the Black Country*), whereas *Perth and Kinross* covers almost three and a half times that in slightly fewer pages. Comparison of two such radically different areas, parts of different countries for most of history, throws into sharp relief the ways in which the built heritage provides evidence for peoples' manners, customs and beliefs. The great glory of Worcestershire is its wealth of middle and later Norman parish churches, many with lavish sculpture, testament to a densely populated landscape and vigorous local lordship in the century after the Conquest, as well as a relative decline in wealth in the later middle ages and early modern period. In Perth and Kinross there is nothing approaching exuberance in any period after that of the Pictish symbol stones and early (eighth- and ninth-century) crosses; everything is more vernacular, simpler, reflecting the smallness of communities and the different scale and traditions of lordship. While both areas notionally used the same liturgical customs — the Use of Sarum — in the later middle ages, the parish buildings in which they were practised were so radically different that one wonders how much the experience really had in common. After the Reformation there was little new church building in Worcestershire or elsewhere in England, as medieval churches were more or less adapted to the Church of England's varying forms of liturgy. In Scotland, where the established church was fully Protestant, a larger number of radical alterations were carried out (as at St John's Parish Church, Perth, where the building was too large for a single preacher to be heard and was therefore divided into three to enable each of three congregations to hear its own preacher) and rather more churches were rebuilt as preaching spaces. The difference in the nature of the established church is again reflected in the later history of the ecclesiological movement, for the Aberdeen (later Scottish) Ecclesiological Society was not founded until 1886, nearly half a century after the Cambridge Camden Society, and was aimed at reforming a Presbyterian rather than an Anglican church: notable amongst the Perthshire examples inspired by it are the fittings of Dunkeld Cathedral (1908: only the medieval chancel was and is still in use) and the addition of a chancel to the 1790s parish church at Longforgan (1899–1900).

The greatest contrast between *Worcestershire* and *Perth and Kinross* is in their introductions, both over a hundred pages long. *Perth and Kinross*, in common with many of the Scottish series, takes a more historical approach, telling a story, showing how the buildings fit into a bigger picture within and beyond the counties covered. *Worcestershire*, by contrast, is more narrowly architectural: the main sections of the introduction are chronological, and subdivisions on building types being arranged in varying order depending on which type of building provides the best narrative of architectural style and development in the period under consideration. While both approaches are valid, and different readers will have different preferences, one wonders to what extent that adopted in *Worcestershire* was determined by the earlier edition, and whether someone making a fresh start with today's research questions and approaches in mind would have taken a different course, or whether the altogether larger scale of the English series renders problematic the approach adopted in *Perth and Kinross*. Whatever the reason for the difference, while *Worcestershire* admirably fulfils everything one expects from the *Buildings of England* series, and is a great improvement on its predecessor, its introduction is outshone by the way in which that for *Perth and Kinross* contextualises the gazetteer, excites, and gets under the skin of the architectural history of the area.

P. S. Barnwell, Kellogg College, University of Oxford

Philip Baxter, *Sarum Use: The ancient customs of Salisbury*. Spire Books, 2008, 118 pp., 15 col. plates, 19 b&w plates, £12.99 pbk, ISBN 978 1 904965 18 3.

**Sarum Use**
The ancient customs of Salisbury
Philip Baxter

'Sarum Use' is common parlance among those interested in medieval church history, architecture and worship, and to an extent a much maligned, even misunderstood, term. In broad terms, as Philip Baxter points out, it describes the whole pattern of life and worship at Salisbury Cathedral in the late Middle Ages. But its post-medieval treatment has clouded that description. For high-churchmen of the nineteenth-century, the Use of Sarum was the foundation of the ideal of 'the English Church' (Ecclesia Anglicana), a Church that could recover its medieval richness and ethos, but was definitely separate from Rome: that is to say, the Church in England and Wales under Henry VIII and Edward VI from 1534 to 1549. It was the ideal of Church to which many early members of this Society's predecesor aspired. To achieve their ends, these high-churchmen endeavoured liturgically to reconcile late medieval ritual to the texts and rubrics of The Book of Common Prayer (with Merbecke's music for the 1549 Prayer Book as one resource). Their heritage is now best seen in the churches and furnishings they restored or built anew on medieval principles.

In setting up the Use of Sarum as the model for Ecclesia Anglicana, its place within the family of local and regional liturgical Uses that made up the Latin Rite in the West was deliberately not emphasised. Rather its distinctiveness and authenticity was stressed. In fact the Use of Sarum was an extraordinary phenomenon in its own time: in the later Middle Ages it became the normative liturgical Use in the majority of churches throughout England, Wales and Ireland, in parts of Scotland and even in some places outside the British Isles. The exceptions were the dioceses of Hereford and York with their own local Uses and the monastic churches. However, while the liturgical Use was widespread it required adaptation almost everywhere to the buildings and resources of the individual church. Later rubrics are often careful to state what happens in the cathedral church of Salisbury, with the clear expectation that there may be a different way of doing this elsewhere.

Salisbury was particular among the medieval English dioceses. Often we are tempted to simplify them into just two categories – those with cathedrals staffed by either monastic or secular clergy. The picture is, in fact, more complex. Salisbury was originally one of those dioceses with two centres (Sherborne and Ramsbury) with both monastic and secular cathedrals, along with Bath and Wells, and Coventry and Lichfield. Not only did Salisbury become a diocese with a single cathedral after the Norman Conquest, that cathedral was relocated, like Chichester which was moved from Selsey. Salisbury went a stage further, and the cathedral was moved a second time from Old to New Sarum. Each move forced on the cathedral community a re-appraisal of how it should set about life and worship. The codification of practice emerged in two stages marked by two key documents: the Consuetudinary that brought together the practice at Old Sarum around 1200, just before the move down the hill;

and the Customary of the fourteenth century which represents the practice of the cathedral community settled into its new building.

All this preamble is relevant to the understanding of Philip Baxter's book. If you are seeking a clear introduction and guide to medieval worship following the Use of Sarum, this is not it – although it is much needed. If you are seeking a concise history of the cathedral's formation and constitutional and social history, this is not it – although it too would be valuable. But if you want to engage with a more holistic view of the Use of Sarum, that regards the Use as historical but which resonates in our own time, that examines the principal features of medieval worship and reflects something of the complexity and interweaving strands of cathedral life and worship, then this book meets that need. After some background on the broader history and life of the cathedral, the main sections address the calendar, procession, mass and divine office. The last four sections deal with the later history ending with 'Sarum today'. This short and accessible book is written with affection and enthusiasm by someone who has engaged directly with the liturgy (and the chant in particular) as a practitioner. In some ways it reflects that nineteenth-century tendency to connect the medieval with the modern, though of course in the context of a Church that is far more flexible and of our own century.

John Harper, International Centre for Sacred Music Studies

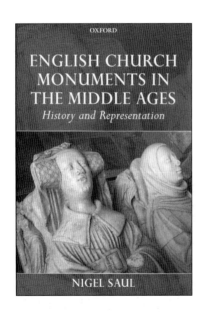

Nigel Saul, *English Church Monuments in the Middle Ages: History and Representation*. Oxford University Press, 2009, 438 pp., 78 b&w pls, £50 hdbk, ISBN 978 0 19 921598 0.

The churches and cathedrals of England contain an astonishing wealth of funerary monuments from the centuries before the Reformation, which have long attracted the attention of antiquaries and church historians, who have recorded their inscriptions, heraldry and costume. In recent times art historians have commented on the sculptural qualities of these monuments, and have attempted to classify the many kinds of memorials that were produced in the medieval era. Now Nigel Saul, in a work of impressive scope and scholarship, has raised the study of medieval monuments to a new level, integrating it into the social history of the middle ages, and making an extremely strong case for this subject to be accepted as a major way of understanding the changing social, cultural and religious assumptions of medieval England. Saul downplays the art-historical appeal of these memorials in favour of the information they communicate about such matters as the relative merits of the clerical and secular ways of life, the innumerable means by which status and honour were sought, the role of the monument in the negotiations between the living and the dead, between the terrestrial life and the life everlasting. A strong theme in this book is the idea that the monument was engaged in a perpetual discourse between the viewer and the deceased, between those who had power to pray and those who sought prayer, and who had invested in stone and brass to record their existence and express their hopes of a continued, fulfilled existence hereafter.

Although a rich repository of tombs remains, it is nowhere as complete as it once was. Nigel Saul reminds us that the dissolution of the monasteries caused the loss of a vast number of monuments of high-status ecclesiastics, such as abbots and priors, along with members of the nobility and benefactors, who regarded monasteries as the holiest and securest places to be buried. We learnt that city churches, particularly in London, York and Bristol, were usually of modest size, yet much in demand for the interment of wealthy citizens; they were subject to periodic clear-outs and tidyings-up, in which the earlier medieval monuments were often removed. The Fire of London incinerated a world of fine memorials. Saul estimates that before the Civil War, there at least 2500 monuments in London, of which fewer than 2% survive.

All significant social groups developed their distinctive form of monument. We learn to recognise the characteristic representations of the ancestrally-encumbered aristocracy, the various grades of the gentry, the higher and lower clergy, scholars and merchants. Saul sensibly includes brasses in his conspectus, rather than treating them as a class of memorial to be separately studied, as has often been the case. Every aspect of the monumental scene is rewardingly explored here. We learn of the fashions for various kinds of stone in different eras, the modes of production, transport and assembly, and we learn much about the process of commissioning tombs and their cost from contracts that have survived. The deceased and his family usually had a decisive input into the style, decoration and inscriptions of the tomb. Saul draws attention to the periodic assertiveness of certain classes: he documents the collective glory of the military elite during the time of the Hundred Years War, the increasing honour of the legal profession in the fifteenth century, and the rise of the wool merchants in the later middle ages. Episcopal tombs were always prominent, for bishops understandably used the noble setting of their cathedrals to declare the unique authority of their office.

Many hundreds of monuments from all parts of England are drawn into the discussions of this book, which is clearly the work of many years of observation and thought. This is a most enlightening addition to a dark subject, and it will enlarge the understanding and sharpen the eyes of all medievalists.

Graham Parry, University of York

David King, *The Medieval Stained Glass of St Peter Mancroft, Norwich.* Oxford University Press, 2006, 228 pp., 25 col. plates, 187 b&w plates, £99.00 hdbk, ISBN 978 0197262 64 1.

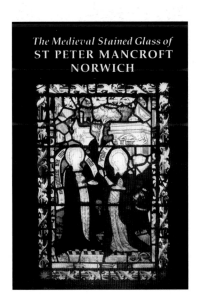

St Peter Mancroft, dominating the southern edge of the market place, is the most important parish church in the city of Norwich. The quality and quantity of surviving stained glass from its fifteenth-century glazing schemes make it the touchstone for Norfolk glass of the period. The medieval city was one of the greatest in England, and the largest guildhall outside of London was erected on the opposite side of the market during the rebuilding of the present church. Norwich was second only to York in its production of stained glass. While other centres of production did exist in Norfolk, most of what survives in the county derives from the city. The style of the stained glass being produced in Norwich in the fifteenth century has been favourably contrasted with the work of court glaziers, and is much admired for its lively painting and use of colour. The present volume provides a definitive account of this key monument and shines a light on the medieval glaziers' craft.

Since the establishment in 1956 of the British section of the CVMA (*Corpus Vitrearum Medii Aevi*), this project has published a dozen volumes surveying the medieval stained glass of particular counties and individual sites as well as the popular format type of the roundel. The present full (rather than summary) catalogue is the first in the British series of publications to focus on the glazing of a single parish church. The author, David King, speaks from a unique position of authority on the subject. He was born into a family of glaziers based in Norwich, whose studio specialised in the restoration of medieval stained glass, operating on an unprecedented scale in the aftermath of World War II. As an art historian, King has published widely on the medieval stained glass of Norfolk. One of the chief interests of the present volume is the appendix of biographies of medieval glass painters working in Norwich. Further appendices bring together the relevant documentary evidence and antiquarian records, making them available for further scrutiny and study. The brief accounts of the wider context of the glazing at St Peter Mancroft whet the appetite for the author's next project to produce a survey of the surviving medieval glass across the county. While the summary catalogue for Norfolk is awaited with due anticipation, this volume contains more than enough material with which to while away the time.

Rosie Mills, Victoria and Albert Museum

Roger Rosewell, *Medieval Wall Paintings in English and Welsh Churches*. The Boydell Press, Woodbridge, 2008, 384 pp, 255 col. plates, 6 b&w plates, £39.95 hdbk, ISBN 978184 3833680.

This book is an enticing introduction to a fascinating subject, a visual feast with an eminently readable text. Its author, Roger Rosewell, is a professional journalist with a scholarly enthusiasm for medieval wall paintings, known to many as the energetic and tenacious editor of the Corpus Vitrearum's email newsletter *Vidimus*. His profusely illustrated book is an invitation to explore, being equipped with a gazetteer of over 500 locations, a subject index and a long and up to date bibliography which will be a valuable tool for many readers. On page 5 he sets out his agenda: When were the paintings made? What do they show? Who made them? How were they made? Why were they made? Why did the Church stop making them? Where can I see some more?

He successfully answers most of these questions with the assistance of his own and C B Newham's exceptional images, of which figures 213–15, illustrating the cadaver effigy and painted interior of the lower tomb chest of Alice de la Pole, are surely the most spectacular. The book is clearly structured. An introductory history of wall paintings is followed by thematic chapters on subjects, patrons and painters, the making of wall paintings, meaning and understanding and reformation and rescue. A gazetteer of locations arranged in county order and a subject guide are useful tools for those readers wishing to go out in pursuit of the real thing, of which there will surely be many. Rosewell is a natural communicator and the text is refreshing and lively, in which complex issues are discussed in an unpretentious manner which will demystify this fascinating subject for the wide audience for whom the book is clearly intended.

The author does not profess to be a professional art historian or iconographer so it is perhaps no surprise to discover that not all aspects of the subject are treated equally satisfactorily. The authorship of complex narrative schemes – the respective roles of priest, patron and patron – might have benefited from wider discussion and the impact of liturgy on the disposition and location of paintings is not tackled. Nor is there any discussion of the relative popularity of subjects over time, and all church types are treated the same. Dating is rather generalised. Nonetheless, the author covers an enormous amount of ground with a lightness of touch.

Much as this book is to be welcomed, it has its shortcomings, some of which could be addressed in any revised edition. The county location of the sites illustrated is not provided in the figure captions and the sites listed in the gazetteer are not cross-referenced to the illustrations. As there are no footnotes or endnotes, it would also have been useful to include some kind of cross-referencing between the gazetteer and the bibliography, as finding the sources for individual schemes discussed or described entails a laborious slog through the commendably long bibliography. A map would also be very useful.

These caveats cannot detract from the value of the book which will be valuable to scholars and students of church architecture alike.

Sarah Brown, University of York

Ingrid Roscoe, Emma Hardy and M.G. Sullivan, *A Biographical Dictionary of Sculptors in Britain, 1660–1851.* Yale University Press, 2009, 1620 pp., £80.00 hdbk, ISBN 978 0 300 14965 4.

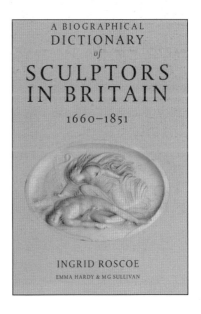

Who carved Nelson, or his lions, in Trafalgar Square? Who created the statue of Shakespeare in Westminster Abbey? Who carved the Albert Memorial? Sculpture in this country rarely receives the attention it merits. In country houses, visitors will look with admiration at paintings and furniture, but the busts and statues get scant notice. In churches, the monuments are all too often seen as a conventional part of the fabric: few are curious about their makers. In public places, statuary is taken for granted. Britain is dense with sculpture, but we need much more information about its creators in accessible form in order to promote appreciation and understanding.

The foundation stone of a fuller understanding of the nation's sculptural inheritance has been laid with the publication of this remarkable work of reference. Hitherto the main resource for British sculptural history has been Rupert Gunnis's *Dictionary of British Sculptors, 1660–1851*, last updated in 1968, which was a valiant solo performance that gathered as much as was known about the artists and their oeuvre. Gunnis acknowledged that his work was only a beginning. Now it has been used as the basis of a vastly expanded volume, an archive in itself, produced under the patronage of the Paul Mellon Centre and the Henry Moore Foundation. Ingrid Roscoe, known particularly for her work on Peter Sheemakers, has done a superb job as principal editor and compiler, with outstanding support from Emma Hardy and M. G. Sullivan. Many of the major entries are by scholars who have already written extensively about their subjects. The volume is testimony to the enormous advances in art-historical research in the last forty years. Now we have biographical information on over 3000 British sculptors with lists of their works, and details of location and costs and relevant documentation. Foreign sculptors working in Britain are of course included. Entries range from men with only a solitary documented piece to figures who carved enough marble to fill St Paul's. Since much of a sculptor's oeuvre often consisted of funerary monuments, that category is given pride of place; as an aid to research into church monuments, the details provided here are invaluable. For a conspectus of the achievements of Nost or Nollekens, Edward Baily or Thomas Banks, Chantrey or Westmacott, enquire within. This volume immediately establishes itself as the indispensable companion to sculptural studies: it is, appropriately, a monumental work of scholarship.

Graham Parry, University of York

## Other publications received

Mary Berg and Howard Jones, *Norman Churches in the Canterbury Diocese*. The History Press, 2009, 208 pp., 33 col. plates, 70 b&w plates, £20.00 pbk, ISBN 978 0 7524 4776 6.

William the Conqueror's arrival here in 1066 brought with it a transformation of English society and culture. Nowhere more visibly is this change reflected than in church architecture, particularly in the Canterbury diocese of East Kent, an area rich in churches of the Norman period.

During the twelfth century around 100 churches were built or re-built in the eastern half of Kent and the authors shed light on why the work was undertaken, the materials and construction methods used, how much the churches cost, how they were paid for and by whom. The book explores the close links between east Kent and the Bessin area of Normandy around Bayeux and Caen, which started with William the Conqueror's half brother, Ode the Bishop of Bayeux, later to become earl of Kent. Suggestions are put forward about how these links were strengthened and then, after 1204, broken. Political and social developments are reviewed as well as the architectural background.

The book includes studies of the 18 principal churches in the diocese and a gazetteer of related buildings. It also contains helpful plans, line drawings and photographs.

# The Ecclesiological Society

The Ecclesiological Society is for all those who love churches, and are interested in their fabric, furnishings and use. The Society was founded in 1879, as a successor to the Cambridge Camden Society of 1839. It has a lively programme, including various lectures, an annual conference, and visits to churches at a range of locations in the UK. Members receive the Society's periodical, *Ecclesiology Today*, twice a year.

Membership is open to all. For further details, see the Society's website at www.ecclsoc.org, or write to the Hon. Membership Secretary at the address given overleaf.

## Contributions to *Ecclesiology Today*

The Editor is always pleased to receive articles for consideration for publication in *Ecclesiology Today*, or suggestions for proposed contributions, whether fully worked out or at an early stage in development. The Society wishes to encourage less-experienced authors, and the Editor is happy to provide informal support and guidance to those in this position.

In furtherance of the Society's aims, articles should promote 'the study of the arts, architecture and liturgy of the Christian Church'. They may be historical in nature, or reflect contemporary matters. They need not be restricted in time, place or denomination, and although in practice a significant number deal with Church of England churches, in recent years a wider range of material has been covered, a trend which it is wished to encourage. Articles dealing with individual buildings are welcome, although the Editor will expect the discussion to highlight matters of wider significance. The Society's interests cover a very wide field, and it is therefore important that articles should be written in a way which can be understood by anyone with a general interest in churches.

Most articles are objective and factual, but there is the opportunity for well-argued personal views on matters of general interest to be put forward in the occasional 'Viewpoint' series.

Prospective authors are invited to communicate with the Editor at the earliest possible stage. There is no formal process of refereeing, but articles will often be sent to one or more readers for an independent opinion before acceptance for publication, and eventual publication may be dependent upon the author making such modifications as the Editor, in consultation with the readers, may recommend.

Proposed contributions should preferably be submitted by email. They should be prepared in accordance with the style guide, available on the Society's website or by application to the Editor. Authors are reminded that they are responsible for any fees and permissions required for the reproduction of illustrations.

Books for review should be sent to the Reviews Editor. Material for *Church Crawler* should be sent to the News Editor.

# The Ecclesiological Society